"Our ability to accessorize is what separates us from the animals."

OLYMPIA DUKAKIS *in "Steel Magnolias"*

CHIC
SIMPLE ®

ACCESSORIES

THAMES AND HUDSON

THIS IS A BORZOI BOOK
PUBLISHED BY ALFRED A. KNOPF. INC.

First published in Great Britain in 1996
by Thames and Hudson Ltd. London
Reprinted in 1996

KIM JOHNSON GROSS JEFF STONE

WRITTEN BY CHRISTA WORTHINGTON
ART DIRECTION BY WAYNE WOLF
PHOTOGRAPHS BY JAMES WOJCIK

STYLE DIRECTION BY AMANDA MANOGUE BURCH
STYLING BY ADAM GLASSMAN AND HOPE GREENBERG
CHAPTER ILLUSTRATIONS BY LAURA LJUNGKVIST
ILLUSTRATIONS BY GREGORY NEMEC
ICON ILLUSTRATIONS BY AMY JESSICA NEEDLE
HANGER AND FIRST AID ICONS BY ERIC HANSON

British Library Cataloguing-in-Publication Data

A catalogue record for this book is available from the British Library

ISBN 0-500-01708-5

Printed and bound in the United States of America

Thank you to those who gave me my lifelong favorites:

KID
- red Keds
- red patent Mary Janes

TEEN
- a wooden-handled purse with a button attached, embroidered linen cover
- navy quilted bag with silk scarf tied to the shoulder strap
- gold bangle bracelets
- gold charm bracelet
- big, colorful plastic and papier-mâché jewelry
- arm bracelets that rested above the elbow
- chain-link belts
- hairpieces
- platform sandals
- liquid eyeliner
- Pappagallo shoes

COLLEGE
- clogs
- L.L. Bean moccasins
- L.L. Bean duffel
- espadrilles
- big straw shoulder bag
- little gold hoop earrings

POST-COLLEGE
- my mom's closet (Kenneth Jay Lane, Pucci, Gucci, and Hermès treasures)
- Arpège by Lanvin (thank you, Dad)

MARRIAGE
- engagement ring and wedding band (thank you, David)
- diamond studs
- pearl necklace (thank you, Mort & Toby)

CAREER
- Belgian loafers
- Birkenstock sandals
- Manolo Blahnik heels
- big black totes: summer and winter versions
- Timex watch
- Kazuko pin
- cheap black sunglasses with UV protection
- Cartier tank watch
- lipstick
- big gold hoop earrings
- black satin evening bag (major thrift shop find)

And what amazes me is that I still wear them all—except for my red Keds,
which my youngest daughter now wears.

K. J. G.

Whatever.

J. S.

For Titi.

C. W.

"The more you know, the less you need."

AUSTRALIAN ABORIGINAL SAYING

CHIC
SIMPLE

Chic Simple is a primer for living well but sensibly. It's for those who believe that quality of life comes not in accumulating things but in paring down to the essentials. Chic Simple enables readers to bring value and style into their lives with economy and simplicity.

C O N T

HOW TO USE THIS BOOK: Understanding the important quality points of accessories is the basis of the Chic Simple philosophy of developing personal style. The fashion-savvy woman understands the significance and the appropriateness of what she's wearing. To make it simpler, we created the following system of icons, which flag contextual information in graphic shorthand. We've also provided another aid in the chapter opening: the basic wardrobe list in each section is yours for the checking. And on the pages labeled "simple lesson" we illustrate how various accessories can transform a given outfit.

BASIC. Survival gear, must-haves, or just the BASIC wardrobe building blocks, these are the essential items that will allow you a lifetime of pleasure and value when carefully selected. They're the kinds of things you borrow from your mother and somehow never return.

BODY. This icon indicates an item that is flattering to a certain BODY type but perhaps not to others. As in all broad generalizations, there will be exceptions to the rule—so read with one eye cocked at the mirror.

COLOR. This icon calls attention to a color issue—both when it's used to flexible, wardrobe-expanding advantage and when it's used to add sizzle.

DRESS CODES. Remember when you got sent home for wearing clogs or punk jewelry to school (or work)? With the dress-down Friday becoming a weeklong phenomenon, DRESS CODES are now more about appropriateness—the what, when, where questions.

PATTERNS. In general, most of us would look better if we avoided PATTERNS. Chintz is tough to pull off; however, a judicious use of classic prints is another way of adding vitality to the basics.

PROFILE. Throughout the long journey of style there are certain individuals, companies, and even products that stand out as important design milestones.

SIMPLE TRUTHS. Wisdom and pieces of advice that help make life simpler. It's a fact: earrings shouldn't weigh more than your head, and other clarifications that will aid you in their simple consistency.

TEXTURE. Material or surface treatment can add to an accessory's visual and tactile impact. A neck scarf, sensible in knit, becomes a flirtatious layering in silk. A shimmering organza with everyday wool creates drama.

VALUE. When purchasing accessories, it is important to invest in VALUE. A handbag might cost $500, but if it is of high quality and classic design, so that you can carry it five times a week all year long, it's actually costing you less than $2 per use for that year.

VERSATILITY. How easily can an accessory mix and match with a variety of wardrobe fundamentals? This icon doesn't mean you can use it to dry the dog and polish the silverware, but with just a change of earrings you may be able to wear it to the office and on a blind date that night.

E   N   T   S

SIMPLE ADDITIONS

"Your mother never had a sense of style. Her dolls were always half naked and mine were perfectly groomed.... I gave her my prescription to dress for success.... Accessories are the key to fashion. Tessie honey, you can wear real junk...but with the right earrings, bracelet and scarf you will always be very 'too-too.'"

GORGEOUS *in "The Sisters Rosensweig,"*
a play by Wendy Wasserstein

SIMPLE ADDITIONS

☐ BAG
☐ BELT
☐ BRACELET
☐ BUTTONS
☐ CUFFLINKS
☐ GLASSES
☐ EARRINGS
☐ GLOVES
☐ HAIR ACCESSORY
☐ HAT
☐ NECKLACE
☐ PIN
☐ RING
☐ SCARF
☐ SHOES
☐ STOCKINGS
☐ WATCH

ak-se

AN ARTICLE

s - a - r e

OF DRESS THAT COMPLETES OR ENHANCES ONE'S OUTFIT.

WHERE TO START?

1. TAKE INVENTORY

2. DEJUNK AND SHOP YOUR WARDROBE

3. REDISTRIBUTE AND REINVEST YOUR ASSETS

1. Scan your closet with a laserlike gaze. Home in on what you like to wear and wear most often. These are your basics. A black dress. A tailored suit. 2. Weed out the inessentials. Clothes that don't work, that are never worn, that don't make you happy. Then do the same with accessories. To wear small things well you must organize them. Sort bracelets, earrings, and necklaces together in ways you'd most likely wear them—gold with gold, for instance. Half the art of wearing accessories is being able to lay hands on them on impulse. Use transparent storage devices—tackle boxes or see-through plastic wardrobe bags with zip-up pockets. 3. Now that you know what works, you know better where to spend your money. Imagine new ways to accessorize the clothes you wear most.

"I love America, and I love American women. But there is one thing that deeply shocks me—American closets. I cannot believe one can dress well when you have so much."

ANDRÉE PUTMAN

LEOPARD-SKIN PURSE

It's just big enough to hold the essential instruments of charm. Lipstick. Hanky. Keys. Comb. Cab fare. Yet it makes a dramatic statement by force of pattern—racy spots set the tune for an entire outfit; a mood for day or night.

CANVAS TOTE BAG

Conceived by L.L. Bean in 1944 as an "ice carrier" for stocking the icebox, the canvas tote was reissued in the sixties as the "Boat and Tote Bag" and made nautical-looking with two colors.

ACCESS NOT EXCESS

"ACCESSORY" IS A MISNOMER WHEN IT COMES TO DESCRIBING THIS STRATEGIC ELEMENT OF THE MODERN WARDROBE. IN THE AGE OF THE UNIFORM, THE SO-CALLED EXTRAS

have become points of access to style. With today's simplified silhouette, accessories demand attention and have become more determining of one's style—as individual as the look in one's eye or a laugh. If you have command of accessories, you tap into something powerful—the image of the person you are, or that you want to be. When the late, great *Vogue* editor Diana Vreeland posed for a photograph, her cashmere top served as a backdrop for an ivory-tusk necklace shaped like a lurid half moon or a dangerous banana. She was a Boadicea, a Druidic goddess, not just a little lady in a cashmere sweater. Style, she knew, was in the details—the sweet exaggeration.

BANKABLE STYLE. Investing in accessories requires equal parts realism and fantasy. Dress for the life you have, as well as the life you want to lead. Strategize expenditure. The more costly pieces should be the most adaptable and immune to trend: black shoes, pearl studs. The beauty of accessories is that they don't have to blow the bank. The fashionable material, color, or pattern can refresh a wardrobe. A leopard-print bag, in any material, is a racy classic, a thrill, evocative of *La Dolce Vita* and nights that lead into dawn. Go ahead. Dream of Marcello Mastroianni and wiggle on the wild side, even if you wake up in Kansas.

DAY
Function with pep:
The backpack and
baseball cap. Jaunty
but classic sneakers.

NIGHT
The shock of pink.
Surfaces that shimmer.
Jewelry in translucent,
edible colors. Sexy
spots: mules that reveal
the heel; patent leather
at the waist.

BASICS + ACCESSORIES = **VERSATILITY**

Casual straw and slip-on
sandals relax the basic
white shirt and dark pants,
and create an adult style of
playfulness.

URBAN

Sturdy oxfords. Leather
that can take spit and
polish. Elegant but mini-
mal jewelry. Womanly
shades. A spot of color.

Economics 101. The more wear you can get from basics, the more valuable and cost-effective they become. Hats, shoes, belts, and bags paint the specifics of season, mood, and moment in the most minimal wardrobe. They let you have the fun of making a statement. The same white shirt and dark pants can reveal multiple personalities, depending on the little things.

The simplest pleasure is a perfectly utilitarian item that is also the best of its kind.

FUNCTION

NECESSITY IS THE MOTHER OF INVENTION.

FOR EVERY ACCESSORY THERE WAS FIRST A

REASON FOR BEING, A HUMAN NEED ATTACHED. A BAG WAS

for carrying stuff bigger than your two hands. An umbrella was mobile shelter. A diamond ring was portable wealth—a dowry that could be passed down through generations. Accessories in this regard were never frivolous. Pins and brooches held capes together before buttons came along.

> "Women shop to look beautiful. Men shop not to look stupid."
>
> **DAVID H. EDWAB,**
> *CEO, Men's Warehouse*

Belts carried swords. The archetypal items survive the centuries because they best suit a purpose. To figure out what accessories you need, first identify the need itself. Do you require a bag to wear dancing or a bag for toting yourself around town all day? Think about it.

CLIMATE CONTROL. Rain, sleet, snow, air-conditioning: the elements have helped shape the evolution of fashion accessories. Items conceived for a specific activity regularly spill over into other daily uses: river sandals, made for wading in riverbeds, have become all-purpose pavement pounders in the few short years since their creation. Uses can also shift slowly, over many fashionable eras. The cashmere shawl has acquired additional purpose in the modern age as a business travel blanket, as well as a ready antidote to excessive air-conditioning in the office.

F O R M

EVEN IN ACCESSORIES, THE IDEA THAT FORM FOLLOWS FUNCTION HOLDS TRUE. STYLE REVEALS ITSELF BY ASSOCIATION. A BACKPACK, AN EMBLEM OF RUGGED ENDURANCE, TURNS

into something altogether differ-ent with the addition of a bamboo handle—the insignia of Gucci, and held, traditionally, by the most pampered hands. This bit of ele-gance can go anywhere, with youthful indiscretions and ath-leticism sanctioned. It is, after all, a backpack. The most eligible archetypes—things that are well

DRESS SACK
Fashion comes to the knapsack in patent leather and a petite discreet shape.

designed—get embroidered upon liberally: dressed up and taken out in new and different, often more luxurious fabrics. This holds true for all the classics of cloth-ing. Style speaks through utility. The line between hiking gear and generic carrier has long since been crossed by the backpack. It has been unisex from its inception.

AFLUTTER

Babe Paley, the late style-setting wife of the founder of CBS, is credited with popularizing—in the sixties—the idea of tying a scarf onto the handle of a handbag in the manner of a flag on the mast of a ship. Photographers captured this sartorial inspiration as Mrs. Paley left La Grenouille, the New York restaurant that has long been a favorite of the social and fashion worlds.

S T Y L E

DETAIL—LIKE IMPERFECTION—BLAZES THE TRAIL TO CHARACTER. IT MAKES PERSONALITY PALPABLE. AS MODERN CLOTHES HAVE ACQUIRED MASS-produced uniformity, accessories have become more strategic as indicators of style. They nail down specifics. They denote time and place. "Formality," for instance, is signaled by the presence of a high heel, a sparkling ornament, the little thing that goes a long way toward defining mood and merriment. Accessories make identifying music; they hum a theme song as you walk into the room. Often, the best tunes are dissonant: a familiar form with a new twist in material, color, or texture. Accessories do a lot of talking, and they invite response. They extend the boundary of the individual, like a handshake.

TREND VERSUS CLASSIC How to adapt a trend to your purpose? Or a classic? First figure out what you want from it. Trend has to do with hormones. Classics calm and reassure; they support any claim to be taken seriously. The shape of a heel, the curve of a toe are fashion indicators that date an entire outfit. The most significant trends introduce new materials. High-tech fabrics—nylon and stretch vinyls—have revolutionized the accessory as much as they have clothing. They are here to stay. The latest is the holograph, which makes a pump look airborne even when it's solid.

WHAT MAKES IT A PUMP?

The term describes the kind of low-cut upper that wraps around the foot and slips on. Evening shoes communicate through subtle signals: a cutaway arch or an ankle strap can alter the tone and temperature. In black they assure elegance. They become a classic. The same form suits different settings depending upon whether it's made of leather, silk faille, or holographic synthetic.

ANKLE STRAP
Avoid ankle straps if ankles are thick.

A trend is more at home on the dance floor; a classic, on the job.

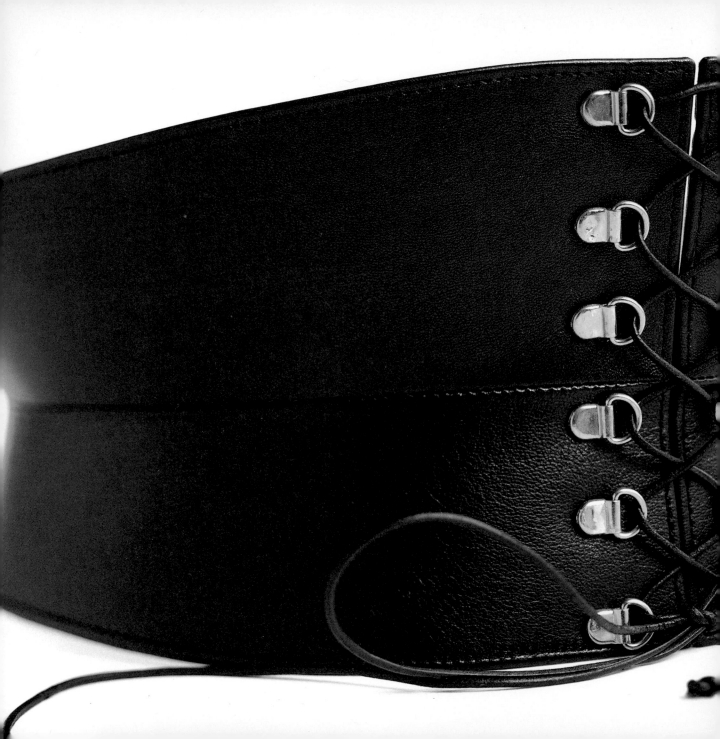

REVEAL AND CONCEAL

GABRIELLE (COCO) CHANEL

HEAPED PEARLS AND GOLD CHAINS DOWN HER NECK TO HIDE HER BODY. IT WAS memorable camouflage, liquid armor. A dazzling mask. She commanded the eye like a hypnotist. Real or imagined flaws can be treated with the cure—the cosmetic nip and tuck—of detail. The corset belt, or corselette, has come out of the closet in recent years to lace the torso into shape. But there are more illusionary methods of trimming inches and lengthening lines. Accessories by nature exaggerate. Give them an inch and they'll take a mile. A wide or thin belt can tip the balance of the body. Each draws a line of color and shape to be reckoned with.

CAMOUFLAGE TACTICS. A wide belt shortens the upper body and works well on most women. A loosely slung belt lengthens the torso. If a belt is the same color as your top, it will visually lower your waistline; matched to the color of a skirt or pants, it has the effect of lengthening legs and shortening the waist. Belts in a contrasting color risk widening and shortening the look of the body—not a problem if you're tall and thin. If your waist is less than slim, you can still wear a buckled belt beneath a cardigan or a jacket as a way of creating the suggestion of a curve without having to prove it.

"Within a year after she moved into the White House, women all across the United States had memorized the high-fashion mathematics of multiplying chic by subtraction."

MARYLIN BENDER
on Jackie O.

IS FOR ANATOMY

THE SHINBONE'S CONNECTED TO THE THIGH BONE...AND ACCESSORIES RECOMBINE LIKE MOLECULES IN AN EXPERIMENT, SPLITTING AND FUSING LICKETY-SPLIT.

How to manipulate the outcome of so many volatile variables? The challenge is to work in close-up while thinking globally. Confining an accessories statement to a single body "zone"—feet, waist, hand, or head—helps make a point. Too much intra-accessory competition is a bad thing.

Exaggerate according to the rules of style math: symmetry is good. A pair of cuff bracelets, one on each wrist, doubles the impact. Learn to lean into extremes, even if it means underaccessorizing.

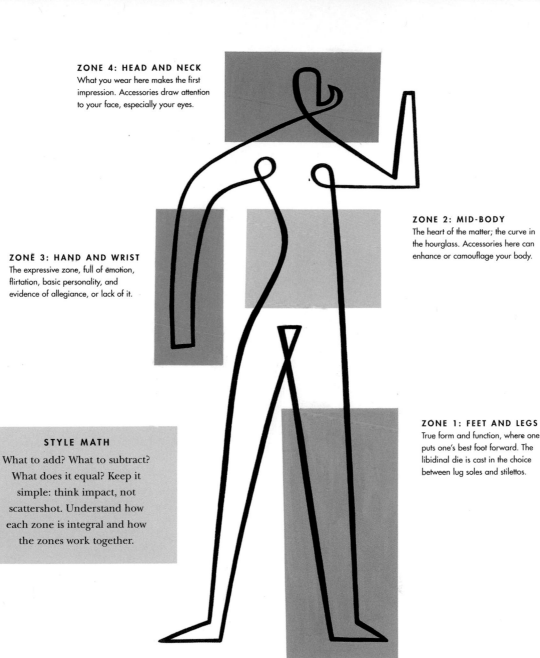

ZONE 4: HEAD AND NECK
What you wear here makes the first impression. Accessories draw attention to your face, especially your eyes.

ZONE 2: MID-BODY
The heart of the matter; the curve in the hourglass. Accessories here can enhance or camouflage your body.

ZONE 3: HAND AND WRIST
The expressive zone, full of emotion, flirtation, basic personality, and evidence of allegiance, or lack of it.

ZONE 1: FEET AND LEGS
True form and function, where one puts one's best foot forward. The libidinal die is cast in the choice between lug soles and stilettos.

STYLE MATH
What to add? What to subtract? What does it equal? Keep it simple: think impact, not scattershot. Understand how each zone is integral and how the zones work together.

Good accessorizing is deciding which one zone you wish to emphasize today.

GROUND FLOOR

"Now Maria pushed the door all the way open, but instead of ushering him inside, she leaned up against the doorjamb and crossed her legs and folded her arms underneath her breasts and kept staring at him and chuckling. She was wearing **high-heeled pumps** with a black-and-white checkerboard pattern worked into the leather. Sherman knew little about shoe designs, but it registered on him that this one was of the moment."

TOM WOLFE,
The Bonfire of the Vanities

ZONE ONE

- ☐ BOOT
- ☐ CLOSED LEATHER PUMP
- ☐ EVENING PUMP
- ☐ LOAFER OR MOCCASIN
- ☐ SUMMER SANDAL: DAY, NIGHT, BEACH
- ☐ SNEAKER

FOOTWEAR

IS, PSYCHOLOGICALLY SPEAKING, THE LIBIDO OF THE WARDROBE. IT EMBRACES FUNDAMENTALS: LIFE FORCE; SEX DRIVE; WHETHER YOU INTEND TO RUN OR WALK.

Once chosen, they determine the mood of what's to come. Be it casual, professional, playful— the big picture is drawn. This makes it easier to get dressed. Shoes affect overall proportion by lengthening the leg, in the case of the high heel, or shortening the calf, as in the case

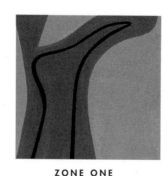

ZONE ONE

The zone with the most outspoken accessory—the shoe. It's voice can drown out all other zones.

of the boot. The more flashy the shoe, the more the eye is pulled down to it. Shoes have to "fit" the hemline of a skirt or trousers and team up with the color and pattern of hosiery. They provide powerful advantages: sex appeal, extra height, and sometimes even comfort.

THE BIG STRETCH. The illusion of leg length is created through the use of monochromatic color schemes and the elimination of pattern or contrast in stockings, socks, and shoes. The more low-cut the shoe, the more flattering it is to the ankle and leg. "A lot of shoe," like a monk-strap shoe that rises to the ankle or an ankle boot, can chop up the line of the leg. **OTHER EYE CATCHERS:** toenail polish, laces, bows, buckles, shiny surfaces.

"Mama always said there's an awful lot you can tell about a person by their shoes: where they're going, where they've been."

TOM HANKS *in "Forrest Gump"*

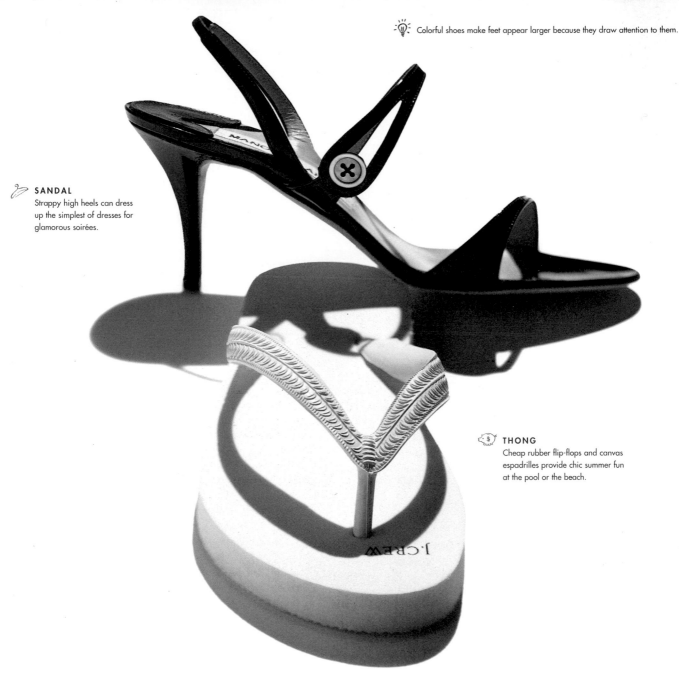

-☼- Colorful shoes make feet appear larger because they draw attention to them.

SANDAL
Strappy high heels can dress
up the simplest of dresses for
glamorous soirées.

THONG
Cheap rubber flip-flops and canvas
espadrilles provide chic summer fun
at the pool or the beach.

[📦 SHOES *first aid—page 154*]

INNER CHILD

Shoes reveal intention. Are you going to kick-start the day or kick back? Choice in a "play shoe" tends to revert to icons of American ease—the sneaker and the cowboy boot. In 1839, Charles Goodyear invented the sneaker when he "vulcanized" (or strengthened) rubber and attached it to canvas shoes. Low-tech sneaker chic has undergone a revival of late, with the worn-out sneaker enjoying a special place of honor. The cowboy boot is more working-class hero: built to last. It has gained street "cred" with heels made to hit the pavement as well as the saddle.

JACK PURCELL SNEAKERS Thick crepe soles, fat laces, sidewalls, and goofily wide bumpers give these low-tech classics the appeal of a Saint Bernard. Made by Converse for the star badminton player in the 1930s, the Jack Purcell is inherently happy-faced.

HOW LONG? For a **6**-eyelet sneaker, 36 inches **7**-eyelet, 40 inches **8**-eyelet, 45 inches **10**-eyelet, 63 inches **12**-eyelet, 81 inches

VINTAGE RODEO
Cowboy boots came into
their own in the late 1800s,
when German immigrant
bootmakers in Texas crafted
them for cowboys who came
through town on six-month
cattle drives and ordered
ahead. Originally, they were
made exclusively for riding
and were too tight and high-
heeled to walk in easily. With
the advent of the performing
cowboy—the rodeo rider—
the heels dropped and the
boots were modified to suit
various rodeo feats.

Outer Adult. At work, you want to wear what works: comfortable shoes. "Those look comfortable" is the kind of compliment welcomed from colleagues and sends out the message that you're "solid." If you're visibly harassed by your shoes, you look inefficient.

FERRAGAMO. Since 1978, Ferragamo's famous "Vara" shoe has flourished on the strength of the mixed metaphor—sporty and elegant with a mid-high heel and its trademark flat grosgrain bow.

LUG SOLE

GUCCI

LOW VAMP

SPECTATOR

J. P. TOD'S
DRIVING SHOE

PENNY

NORWEGIAN PEASANT
SLIP-ON

L O A F E R S

Truly relaxed footwear always maintains composure—like the loafer, a professional lounge act, a loiterer par excellence. Collegiate society (all those football games and frat parties) provided the loafer's initiation into the culture of leisure. It learned well. Be unisex. Be sporting. Be ready for anything. Carry spare change. Have a certain way with jeans and leisure classics like cords. Low-key panache at its finest.

J. P. TOD'S DRIVING SHOE. Diego Della Valle designed this shoe with its rubber nibs across the sole and heel in 1979 for racecar drivers to grip an accelerator. Gianni Agnelli, Fiat chairman, popularized the driving shoe as a patent dress slipper worn with his tuxedo. **LUG SOLE.** This lightweight rubbery outersole adds spring to your walk and provides slip resistance in foul weather. **GUCCI.** In the 1930s, the Italian leather company introduced its loafer in a refined calfskin with a metal snaffle bit across the instep. Now it comes in Technicolor suede, reptile skins, and patent. **PENNY.** Newly casual young Americans in the 1950s popularized this oxblood-colored version of the "Norwegian slipper," making it a coed campus favorite. **LOW VAMP.** The loafer becomes more feminine in soft kid leather and its low cut adds some sex appeal by exposing more of the foot. **NORWEGIAN PEASANT SLIP-ON.** This loafer model was first imported from Scandinavia by American tourists in the 1930s. Then dubbed "weejuns"—a term still used today by Bass. **SPECTATOR.** Two-toned shoes, also known as spectators, in various styles first became popular in the dandy-ish 1920s. In England, such two-toned footwear is called "co-respondent" shoes.

"In the U.S. you have
to be a deviant or die
of boredom."

WILLIAM BURROUGHS

PATENT LEATHER

THE STUFF OF MARY JANES AND TAP SHOES,

PATENT LEATHER IS PLAYFUL FOR ALL ITS SOPHISTICATION.

IT'S SPIFFY AND SWANK, BUT YOUNG AT HEART—A GROWNUP'S TOY.

Developed in the thirties as a waterproof material for shoes, it gives you license to go anywhere. It's the very definition of polish (easily maintained with a soft cloth). Classic in black, it adds surface interest (a dark gleam) to whatever it's worn with. In white,

PATENTLY PERVERSE

In the evolution of the sexy shoe, the world's oldest profession has been key. A New Orleans madam first imported the French high heel to America in the 1880s when she saw how it improved her business. The stiletto is a complex provocatrice: both weapon and precarious perch that tilts the entire body into a "sexy" stance. In them, a woman can stand and fight, but she can't flee. Introduced by Ferragamo in 1952, the stiletto is the most impractical, uncomfortable, spine-threatening shoe. And it's here to stay.

it's positively Twiggyish. Cool and potentially vampish in any color, it's still suitable for church. It has the energy of spring and early summer, even though it's now considered perennial. It re-emerges out of the mists of fashion's cycle in moments of revived glamor.

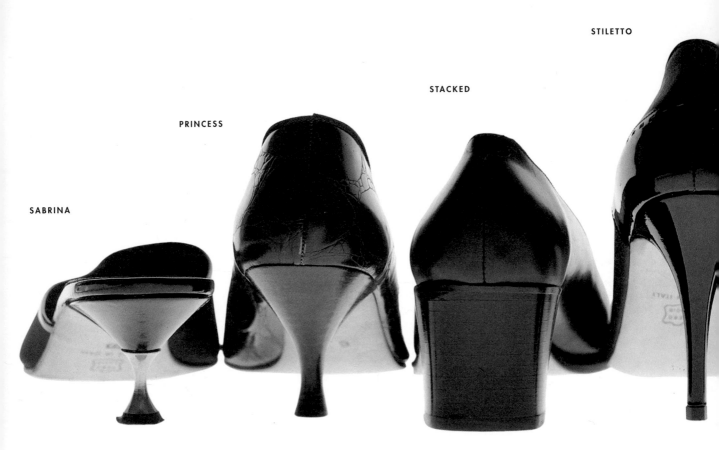

SABRINA PRINCESS STACKED STILETTO

High Heels. There is no more feminizing influence on appearance than high heels. Even the sound of them clicking down a corridor signals "female" a mile off. Like skirt length, heel height is more a matter of taste than dictum. Heel shape is still, however, the trendiest part of a shoe, a bellwether of shifts in style. Often, heel fashion works on the principle of "it's so out, it's in." High heels have been a temptation since the dawn of style. The lead actors of Greek drama towered over their fellow thespians in platform shoes, worn to illustrate, through exaggerated scale, their significance. Men and women wore high heels in seventeenth- and

HIGH STACKED

SENSIBLE

LOUIS

eighteenth-century Europe as a mark of social privilege; only the rich and well-born (the "well-heeled") could afford to teeter above the mud.

The attractions of the high heel are obvious: a swiveling gait, a well-turned ankle, an elongated leg, and added inches—all in all, a daintier foot.

SABRINA. Sweet in an early-sixties, Audrey Hepburn–ish way; fetching on a mule (a backless shoe). **PRINCESS.** The tapered and demure tip of the court shoe. Fine for work and evening dress.

STACKED. Provides height and solid ground. **STILETTO.** A.k.a. the "spike." A force of nature, The sexiest shoe alive, proving the adage that you have to suffer to be beautiful. Turns "walk" into "wiggle."

HIGH STACKED. Stiletto height with better balance. **SENSIBLE.** The legal standard. Traditional. Suitable. **LOUIS.** This distinctive, courtly heel goes through cycles of being very "in" or very "out."

In addition to heel height, the
X-rating of a woman's shoe can
depend on the way it reveals or
conceals "toe cleavage"—where
the toes join the foot—and how
it presents or bares the arch
and the heel.

OBJECT DESIRED

SHOES ARE LARGELY RESPONSIBLE FOR THE

CREDIT-CARD DEBT OF THE AVERAGE WOMAN. HOW IS IT

THAT SOMETHING SO FUNCTIONAL BECAME AN OBJECT OF FOLLY

and fetishistic worship? As the Chinese suspected, it's all to do with the strange sex appeal

of the foot, an appendage that is enticing to tame and toy with, to conceal and reveal. If the

shoe fits, it has something to say about libido. For women, finding the right one is like meet-

ing your prince over and over again. It can be addictive. Shoes are miniature fairy tales.

MANOLO BLAHNIK

Manolo Blahnik doesn't have customers, he has acolytes. Ever since he opened his first shoe boutique in London in 1973, Blahnik has made his name in fantasy and fetish, declaring himself the expert on "toe cleavage." Sex is part of the design motivation behind every pair of boots, pumps, sandals, and signature mules. Blahnik is also adamant about quality: his production process includes one hundred phases and aims for perfection.

REAR VIEW
One of the more provocative angles a shoe can present: a bare heel perched atop a stiletto.

PUMPS
Alligator suggests expense
and elegance. It's a big investment—get a simple style as it
lasts almost forever.

DRESS THONGS
With a heel, the thong
can go to town on summer
days and dance on
summer nights.

MULES
Night creatures. Seductive heel exposure.
Pearls add pizzazz.

STRAPPY HEELS
A black fabric, such as
satin or silk faille, makes a
dressy, if fragile, pump.

after

THONGS
Slip-on comfort and bright color—summer delight.

OXFORDS
The comfort and durability of a man's shoe for women. Handsome with a pantsuit.

ANKLE BOOTS
In the equestrian spirit of the paddock boot, these look great with pants or with skirts when worn with opaque stockings that match the boot leather.

FLATS
Comfort shoes that will work with pants and skirts alike. Chanel introduced this color combination because she believed it flattered the foot.

basic training

PADDOCK BOOT
Originally worn for recreational riding—the paddock boot laces to provide adjustable ankle support—and now a fashion staple. The sole of the authentic riding boot is always sewn, never glued or bonded.

Boot Straps. Boots have masculine energy, an outdoorsy vigor that describes them as essentially casual. Formerly linked to equestrian attire, they fell into fashion in the sixties with the miniskirt. With the leg on show, the boot was made for walking, in a way it hadn't been before. The Courrèges go-go boot and Yves Saint Laurent's thigh-high boot became roguish emblems of freedom. Technology has lately added the comfortable lug sole, and the lightweight hiking boot has infiltrated the wardrobe as plainly as the sneaker. Boots define proportion as decisively as hemlines. They can appear swashbuckling or dainty depending on attitude, heel, and height. All but thigh-high boots draw eyes to the calf. It's up to you to decide if that's where you want to attract attention.

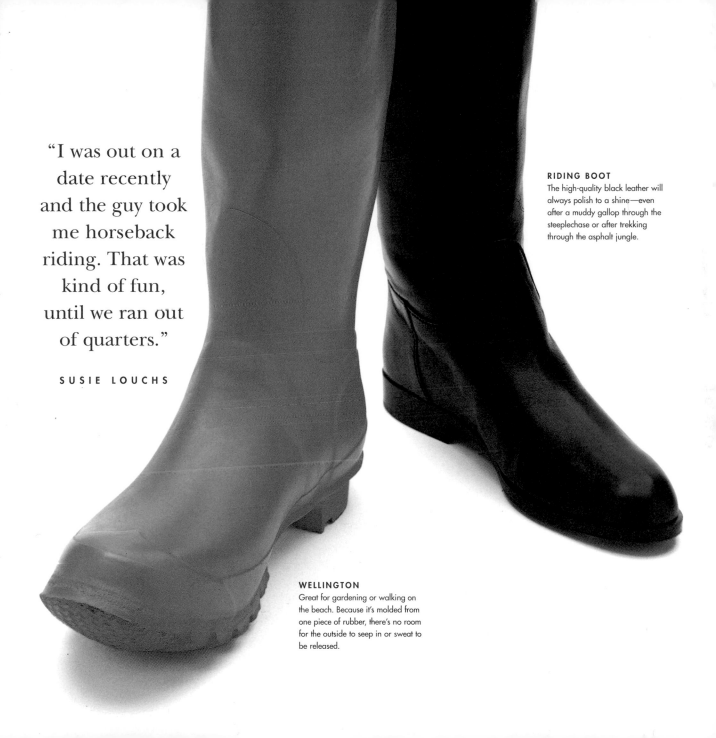

"I was out on a date recently and the guy took me horseback riding. That was kind of fun, until we ran out of quarters."

SUSIE LOUCHS

RIDING BOOT
The high-quality black leather will always polish to a shine—even after a muddy gallop through the steeplechase or after trekking through the asphalt jungle.

WELLINGTON
Great for gardening or walking on the beach. Because it's molded from one piece of rubber, there's no room for the outside to seep in or sweat to be released.

YANG

CHANGE YOUR SHOES AND YOU'VE ESSENTIALLY CHANGED CLOTHES. YOU COULD EVEN ARGUE that style begins at the feet. Shoes can say what clothes can't, without risk of embarrassment: explicit information about mood, such as "I feel all of age 15" or "I'm available for adventure," which could sink the sartorial ship if stated in cloth. Shoes get away with it by working in counterpoint to clothing. A demure dress acquires spirit with racy dancing shoes. A Hollywood mogul can declare herself eternally free to play by wearing juvenile sneakers with a grown-up pantsuit. The message can also play in reverse: spiffy shoes dress up an otherwise relaxed ensemble; quality loafers belie the threadbare casualness of blue jeans. Like the Chinese principles of yin and yang, shoes can round out an outfit's complete story.

"It does not seem fair that, unbeknown to you, every single item you put on your body literally shouts out your subconscious dreams and desires to the entire world."

CYNTHIA HEIMEL, *Sex Tips for Girls*

YANG

The power of the masculine in lace-up oxfords makes the pantsuit authoritative.

YIN

The softer side of city wear: playful sneakers imply that the wearer doesn't need to try that hard.

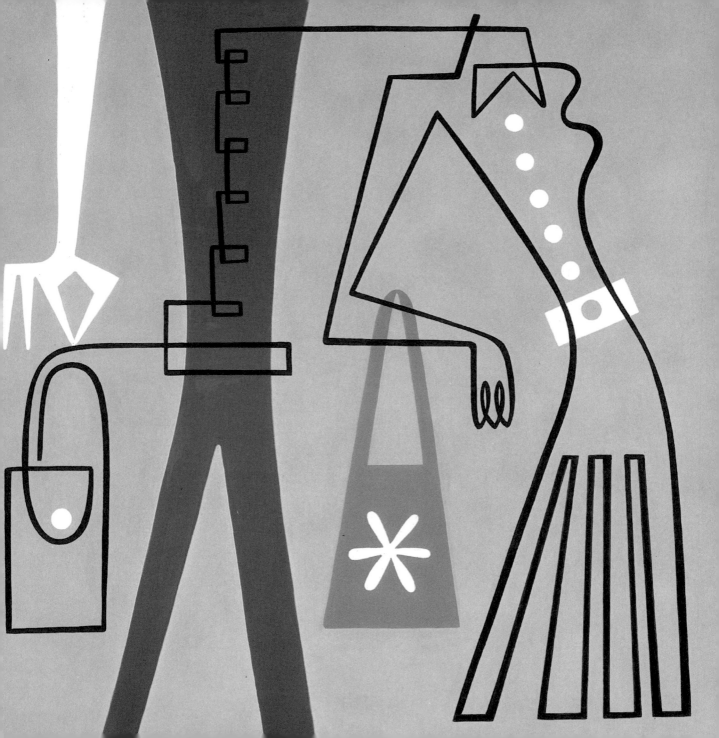

MIDDLEMARCH

62 BELTS 65 BUCKLES 67 HANDBAGS 79 BUTTONS

"Eliminate all handbags. Now look. What have I got here? I carry much more than most people. I've got cigarettes. I've got my lipstick, I've got my comb, I've got my powder, I've got my rouge, I've got my money. But what do I want with a bloody old handbag that one leaves in taxis and so on? It should all go into pockets. Real pockets, like a man has, for goodness sake. Put the money here, lipstick and powder there, the comb and rouge here. Of course, you'd have much bigger pockets, and they'd be rather chic."

DIANA VREELAND

ZONE TWO

- ☐ BLACK OR BROWN LEATHER BELT
- ☐ BUTTONS
- ☐ EVENING CLUTCH
- ☐ GYM BAG
- ☐ HANDBAG
- ☐ TOTE

BAGS AND BELTS

ARE KEY INVESTMENT ITEMS, WORKHORSES THAT GO FAR TO DETERMINE WHAT KIND OF FIGURE YOU CUT. IN A PROFESSIONAL SETTING, THE BAG SIGNALS EFFICIENCY

in the manner of an executive's briefcase. The quality material in a bag or belt works like a letter of recommendation. Shoes and handbags characterize the sensuality and seriousness of the wearer in a way that would seem contradictory were it not for Freud. For him, the handbag was the universal womb. The neat shape suggests smooth performance.

ZONE TWO
While zone two doesn't
have to match zone one,
it must complement it
in spirit.

Proportion is key. A bag should be a bit like you, scaled to your size. Slinky bags on the zaftig look like wishful thinking. Belts are a boon and a bane to the body—camouflage and neon sign—depending on how they are worn. You can allude to a waist even if you don't have one. Buttons help set a standard for clothing, defining it as quality evening or day wear.

HOLDING YOUR OWN. Clutch. Tote. Gladstone bag. Purse. Wallet. Portfolio. Briefcase. Weekend bag. Gym bag. Cinch. Disco belt. Buckle belt. Western belt. Backpack. Handbag. Cosmetic case. Pouch. Drawstring bag. Duffel bag. Pierre Deux bag. Kelly bag. Envelope. Minaudière. Compact. Change purse. Chanel bag. Chain belt. Pocketbook. Pochette. Shoulder bag. Disco bag. Evening bag. Mailbag. Canvas bag. Beach bag. Huntsman's bag. Lunchbox. String bag. Laptop case. Overnight bag.

[BAGS *first aid—page 157*]

CONTOURS

The shapely structured tote becomes elegant in smooth, fine leather. The "constructed" hand-bag made of wood keeps its shape at all times. The most slimming belt has a matching buckle and keepers.

COLOR-CODED

Small colorful bags within a tote bag keep life from being a struggle against entropy. One in blue for cosmetics. One in green for cash. One in red for pens. Organization counts.

Bags and belts without metal hardware complement a greater variety of jewelry.

Belts. Belts help you appear pulled together. They punctuate an outfit as a period does a sentence. In another era, chastity belts ended the discussion. Belts have followed the lines of the silhouette—dropping out of fashion in the twenties, back in with the curvy waist of Dior's New Look in the fifties. Buckles have also appeared on shoes, gloves, and the backs of dresses. The Victorians wore belt buckles with matching brooches in the shapes of lizards, serpents, and butterflies. Material signals degree of formality—a rhinestone buckle against dark suede is a discreet "dressy" statement; a full-metal bejeweled belt dominates and sets the tone for everything worn with it. Silver accents are more casual than gold—Native American concha medallions in silver and turquoise are spectacular but still relaxed. The Western vogue for tooled-leather belts with stamped silver buckles, tips, and keepers serves to camouflage nicks and dents. Chain belts are instantly provocative, perhaps because of the chain's function of keeping things under lock and key. Animal prints and soft suede are sensuous and versatile, allowing you to dress down as you dress up.

CONVERSANT
Certain accessories speak the same language: gold chains and stiletto heels connect in temperament, even though their forms are distinct.

" . . . when I group my clothing according to the traits conveyed, my closet looks like a convention of multiple-personality cases."
ANNA QUINDLEN

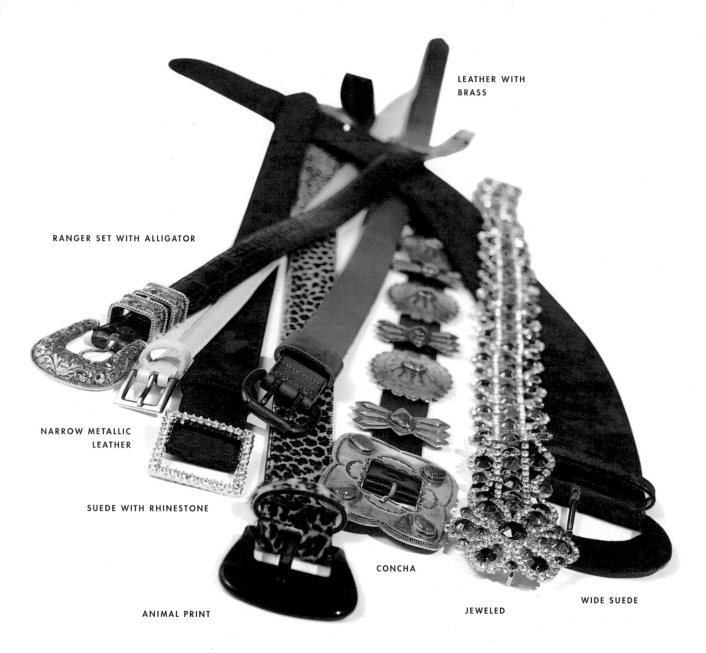

LEATHER WITH BRASS

RANGER SET WITH ALLIGATOR

NARROW METALLIC LEATHER

SUEDE WITH RHINESTONE

ANIMAL PRINT

CONCHA

JEWELED

WIDE SUEDE

To avoid overkill, accessories accompanying decorative belts should be low-key.

TEXTURE
The most basic leather belt thrives on subtle surface interest, such as lizard and alligator skin. Reptile skins are prized for their durability.

Self-colored buckles and keepers enhance the versatility of the belt and make it look tailored.

HANDBAGS

A CITY DWELLER KNOWS SHE HAS ARRIVED IN THE COUNTRY BY THE WAY HER HANDBAG—THE ONE SHE pounds the sidewalks with daily—begins to shriek that it's out of place. Handbags do that. They announce setting, codes of conduct, and the frame of mind of the carrier. They give you away. They transport all the intrigue of mobility—your reason for leaving, your point of arrival. They answer questions: Are you busy? A briefcase. Are

Shape fluctuates with fashion. Generally, the constructed bag is more formal, and looks efficient in the workplace. An overstuffed or bulky bag can make you look disorganized.

A bag has to complement your body. Test shape and size in front of a mirror before you buy, as you would with a pair of jeans. A bag that is too small or too large can distort your presentation. Shorten straps on shoulder bags to optically lift the weight. A shoulder bag that can be slung across your chest relieves strain on the back.

Look for top-grain, not split leather; a leather lining; double-sided straps with no loose threads; and piped and bound seams for strength.

you glamorous? An envelope bag. Are you well defended? A metal minaudière. Are you game? A backpack. Are you adaptable? A soft shoulder bag big enough to hold diapers. Are you status conscious? A designer bag. Could you care less? A plastic shopping bag. Are you determined? A small constructed bag. Worlds in themselves, bags create gestures unique to the female. The hand-held bag makes the body move differently than the one slung across the shoulder. Bags are public display pieces that contain private things: a temptation not only for the thief. As children who steal into Mother's handbag know, it's a place to find out about someone.

ACCORDION PURSE
Functional and feminine, with thin straps
that hold the bag tightly under the shoulder
or let it dangle from the arm.

MINAUDIÈRE
The flirtatious and entertaining metal
minaudière, a signature of Judith
Leiber, is handbag as *objet d'art*.

SILK POUCH
The party pouch. Made for dancing.
Descendant of the reticules of the
nineteenth-century ball.

THE HEIRLOOM BAG
The Gucci bamboo-handled
bag has endured as an emblem of
chic for generations.

SIMPLE CHOICES. Shifting around the
contents of a handbag on a regular basis is
impractical; things are invariably missing just
when you need them. So invest in one that can
go the distance. The essential handbag wardrobe includes: The **EVERYDAY BAG**—
durable, keyed to the setting you most often
operate in, in black or brown leather or a high-
grade man-made fabric such as all-purpose

SOFT TOTE
Relaxed. Functional. Carries work stuff and perhaps a change of clothes.

SHOULDER BAG
The saddlery influence announces itself in the buckle closure and tanned leather flap over no-nonsense nylon.

THE KELLY BAG
The cosmopolitan bag, from Hermès, named for Grace Kelly. The tote of true elegance seconds as a shoulder bag with a detachable strap.

CLUTCH
Slim and elegant in a refined fabric like silk ottoman.

DRAWSTRING TOTE
The touring status symbol, the Vuitton bag, direct descendant of luggage carried only in first class.

STRAW BUCKET
As casual as they come, the scrunchy straw bucket bag is made for summer.

BACKPACK
The nylon backpack, championed by Prada, is in the fabric that has made bags weather resistant, seasonless, ready for anything.

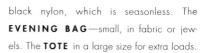

black nylon, which is seasonless. The **EVENING BAG**—small, in fabric or jewels. The **TOTE** in a large size for extra loads.

The **FANNY PACK** or **KNAPSACK** for maximum mobility—black is most versatile. Additional options include the following: The

OVERNIGHT BAG for weekends away and business trips. The **GYM BAG** that can safely segregate your wet and dry clothes.

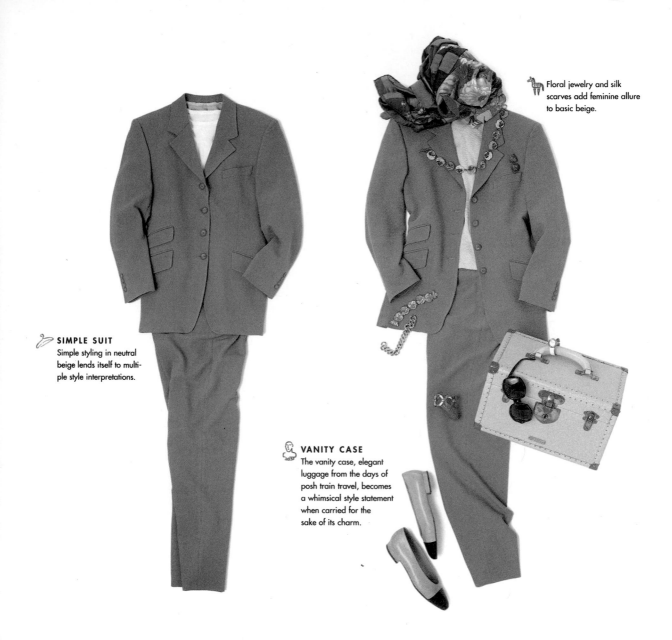

Floral jewelry and silk scarves add feminine allure to basic beige.

SIMPLE SUIT
Simple styling in neutral beige lends itself to multiple style interpretations.

VANITY CASE
The vanity case, elegant luggage from the days of posh train travel, becomes a whimsical style statement when carried for the sake of its charm.

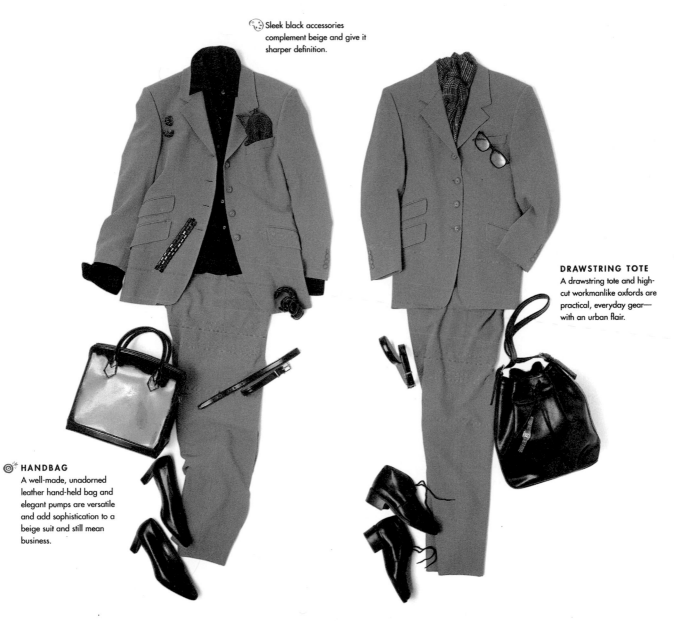

Sleek black accessories complement beige and give it sharper definition.

DRAWSTRING TOTE
A drawstring tote and high-cut workmanlike oxfords are practical, everyday gear—with an urban flair.

HANDBAG
A well-made, unadorned leather hand-held bag and elegant pumps are versatile and add sophistication to a beige suit and still mean business.

purses

QUILTED BAG 1947

CAP-TOE SHOE 1947

COSTUME JEWELRY 1930s

CHANEL

EVEN IN HER OWN TIME, GABRIELLE "COCO" CHANEL DIDN'T MIND THAT HER TASTE IN ACCESSORIES WAS WIDELY COPIED. A GOOD THING, TOO, GIVEN WHAT SHE engendered: Chanelmania. From the dawn of her career in the 1920s, her influence was to release women from the chains of fussy style—ironically, by draping them in chains (well, she was French). She understood the sartorial drama of contrast: opulence against ease, the girlishness of satin bows worn with the boyish sweater, black against ivory—all of it adding up to a new kind of freedom and sex appeal. Accessories assumed their importance to personal style with a built-in simplicity: innovations such as the little black dress, suits with the comfort of sweaters, and cardigan knit "jackets." She mobilized the newly active woman with flat shoes like spectator pumps and sling-backs. She removed the stigma from costume jewelry by using fabulous fakes—splendid imitations of pearls, gemstones, and gold worn with baroque glee. She understood the language of surface: her quilting—on bag, shoe, or bracelet—and the interlocking double-C are as internationally recognized as the *"interdit"* sign.

"I was able to open a high-fashion shop because two gentlemen were outbidding each other for my hot little body."

COCO CHANEL

HOOPS
Large silver hoops, dramatic in themselves, can be worn with any clean-lined, simple necklace.

SILVER CUFFS
The conservative navy suit looks less uptight when worn with silver jewelry.

NYLON POUCH
It can be formal or informal, for business or for play.

BLACK & BLUE
A classic combo. Trying to match navy accessories with a navy suit is often impossible. Black adds sophistication.

PUMPED
Styled like tasseled loafers but with the kind of height necessary to allow women to deal eye to eye with men.

BANGLES
Cufflike bangles make a big impression—more handsome than pretty. They also grip the wrist in a way that keeps you efficient and unencumbered. (That is, if you're not doing your own typing.)

INVESTMENT BAG
The alligator bag—both tote and shoulder bag—delivers indestructible style and quality that should last a lifetime and travel year round. This one is big enough for business.

SCARF
A cashmere scarf in a subtle color is a versatile travel companion that seconds as a blanket in a car or plane.

SHADES
To travel incognito, lenses need a wide girth. The round Jackie O frame keeps the gaze free from eye contact.

tools

A few quality accessories make an impressive presentation.

BLUE AND SILVER BEADS

NYLON

PLASTIC

SILVER MESH

REAL SYNTHETICS

FORMERLY CONSIDERED UNSIGHTLY—NYLON, MESH, AND VINYL—HAVE REVOLUTIONIZED THE TOTE, MAKING IT MORE PRACTICAL AND VISUALLY ENTICING. PLASTIC

has cyberchic as well as unbeatable practicality. Plastic bags are often cheap but they scratch and rip easily—never something worthy of "investment" but definitely worth a kick if it doesn't set you back too much. The great big bag is inherently sporty. In colorful shiny or see-through plastic it becomes a playful focal point—although clear synthetics

MAGICAL MESSENGER BAG

Canvas lined with plastic for strength and waterproofing. As ubiquitous as the fax machine in any urban center, it allows messengers to transport everything from important documents to bulky parcels. If only Hannibal had had them when he crossed the Alps.

discolor to a yellowish tint fairly quickly. Dark nylon is the great crossover handbag fabric—all-purpose for the way it maintains casual as well as urbane cool. Man-made fibers make the ideal tote, gym bag, beach bag, travel bag, and organizer bag-within-a-bag. Like the ubiquitous Baggie, they provide low-cost storage and safekeeping.

INLAY

ABALONE SHELL

BRASS

TARTAN

WHAT'S IN A BUTTON:

Porcelain, ivory, tortoiseshell, pearl, precious metal and jewels, stone (such as marcasite), copper, brass, horn, wood, jade, glass, and plastic. Ivory is now exclusively vegetable. Tortoiseshell is plastic. **"STRASS":** Brilliant paste made of lead glass, used to simulate various transparent gemstones.

PASSEMENTERIE: Trimming of silver and gold threads often interwoven with sequins, pearls, paste, and other glittering materials. **JET:** A hard, compact, coal-related black mineral formed by pressure, heat, and chemical action, popular among the Victorians. Also mimicked with black glass.

JET

MOTHER-OF-PEARL

GRAPHIC

RHINESTONE

BUTTONS

THE UNSUNG ACCESSORY, THE BUTTON DOES MORE THAN ITS SHARE TO ESTABLISH THE APPEAL, SPIRIT, AND PERCEIVED QUALITY OF CLOTHES. INTIMACY IS IN ITS NATURE—IT'S

made to be undone. It makes a personal as well as a public statement. If clothes have fine buttons—real horn, mother-of-pearl from Tahitian mollusks—they are likely to be well made. Those who understand the mood-altering potential of detail know that the right set of buttons can reincarnate an old sweater or dress up a bargain. A basic black cardigan becomes an evening sweater when a standard four-hole plastic button is replaced by jewel or pearl. White buttons tend to be sporting; dark buttons sober. In the twentieth century, designers have used buttons to weigh in with their insignia—Elsa Schiaparelli made them in the forms of tumbling circus acrobats.

CUFFLINKS

Think of cufflinks as decorative detachable buttons. Bold, simple designs of durable materials (silver, enamel, gold) are good investments.

"You press the button, and we'll do the rest."

KODAK ADVERTISEMENT, *c. 1888*

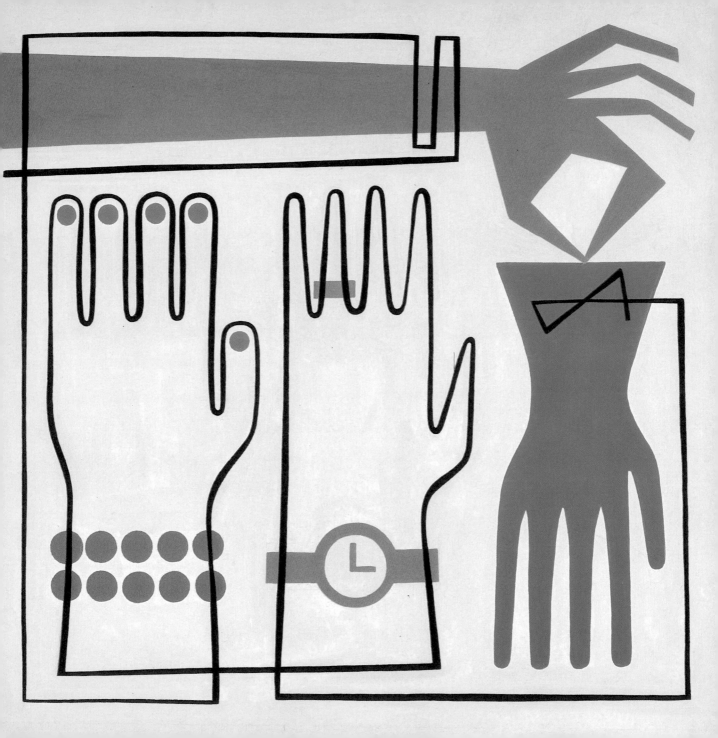

AT ARM'S LENGTH

87 GLOVES 89 BRACELETS 96 WATCHES 98 RINGS

"Anne took off her gloves. She put them into the pocket of her coat, and then got them out again and began to **bite** gently **at** the tip of the third finger on the left one, which was of white cotton and quite dirty and her favorite, because of a lingering agreeable taste of **vanilla** that never seemed to wash away."

M.F.K. FISHER, *"The Boss Dog"*

ZONE THREE

- ☐ GOLD OR SILVER RING
- ☐ BLACK OR BROWN LEATHER GLOVES
- ☐ MANICURE
- ☐ SILVER OR GOLD CUFFS OR BRACELET
- ☐ SPORT WATCH
- ☐ WATCH WITH BLACK OR BROWN LEATHER BAND

HAND AND WRIST

HANDS ARE THE GREAT SIGNIFIERS. FROM THE CARESS TO THE SLAP, THEY TELL A SENTIMENTAL STORY. WHETHER FOLDED AND IDLE OR PLAYING CHARADES, THEY CAN'T

help speaking on behalf of the person attached to them. They animate the soul. Portrait artists pay particular attention to them for this reason. What is worn from fingertip to elbow is a kind of diary for public consumption. The sentimentally significant ring, the wedding band, the anniversary charm are carried like a heart

ZONE THREE

It is the most optional zone, yet it can be the most timely—of the moment (watch) or eternal (wedding band).

on one's sleeve. Hands signal sexual availability in a rather bold fashion, by the presence of rings or the lack of them. They are a source of attraction between the sexes. They are also outfitted for efficiency. This is the "handy" zone, equipped with a watch that works and gloves that keep you functioning despite the cold.

THE BIG PICTURE. Bone structure is the yardstick by which to measure what flatters your own wrist and hand. **WRIST.** A man-sized watch can be sexy on a woman, even if it dwarfs the slightness of her wrist. Bracelets, too, should be scaled to one's proportions. **HAND.** Gloves can be a fashion statement. They set the tone of the entire ensemble by their degree of formality and material. Leather is sporty; slim knits can be more refined. **FINGERS.** Rings highlight the proportions of your hands. Delicate girlish jewelry suits delicate fingers. Chunky rings might be a better choice for those with stouter digits. **FINGERNAILS.** Oval is the more flattering shape. French manicures, which outline the rim of the nail, can be elegant.

[◈ JEWELRY *first aid—page 157*]

SPORTING TRADITIONS
Stitched leather gloves. The choke
collar bracelet in gold. The classic link
bracelet. The gold bangle.

SHHHH...
Jangling jewelry is charming in
some settings, annoying in the
workplace. Take it off before a
concert, ballet, or opera.

TWO-TONE
A bracelet watch in gold and silver
tones is compatible with most jewelry.
It can look dressed up or dressed
down. A good watch makes an
impression in the workplace.

PROPORTION
Long fingers are best suited to
bunched-up rings and dark fingernails. Squared fingernails tend to
make fingers look stubbier.

Jewelry—especially rings and bracelets—can be glamorous when worn in multiples.

GLOVES

FLIRTATIOUS OR FUNCTIONAL, GLOVES ARE THE HATS OF THE HAND. THEY DRAMATIZE INSTANTLY. THEY CAN'T HELP IT. THEY'RE ALL ABOUT MOVEMENT, SO THEY TEND TO provoke. The dropped glove is a mating cry; the gauntlet, a call to combat. Gloves are the first thing to come off in the striptease. They're dangerously seductive, however genteel. Worn as a spot of color or pattern, they create instant style. Dowagers and debs wore them full-length to the ball in a way that made the naked elbow a risqué proposition. They conceal aging hands and attend high tea and church, as well as strip furniture and weed the garden.

> "…gestures of the hand and what's on the hand often can create great theater."
>
> **GEOFFREY BEENE**

THE SIMPLE GLOVE. Find the color and texture and material that you'll get the most use out of and invest accordingly. Don't forget how easy it is to lose gloves: the glove as fashion impulse should be low cost. **BROWN LEATHER GLOVES.** These have the advantage of being casual but tailored. **BLACK GLOVES.** Snug-fitting, in suede, nylon, or cashmere, these are extremely versatile for women with an urban agenda day or night. **EVENING GLOVES.** The most feminine gloves are cut extra low in lace or high up the forearm in velvet. Shimmery fabrics and touches like bows designate evening. **DRIVING GLOVES.** These allow the hand ultimate flexibility and aeration, low cut at the back and buttoned at the wrist. **SPORT GLOVES.** Fingerless weightlifting gloves; boiled-wool rock-climbing gloves; biking gloves. **COLD-WEATHER GLOVES.** Shearling, polyester fleece, or cashmere lined.

CABLE

ANCHOR

BRACKET

IT IS LIKELY TO BE YOUR FAVORITE PIECE OF JEWELRY, THE ONE YOU WEAR every day. The chunky chain bracelet is a classic for the way it maps out continuity and strength by design. Of all bracelets, it's the most versatile while being sculpturally interesting—sporty or formal depending

BRACELETS

on what it's worn with. In the presence of pearls it turns coquettish. Chains also play off each other, with geometrics, curves, and angles that never clash. The baroque appeal of the chain is dramatically heightened in jumbled multiples. The better-made chain— sleek to the touch and with a sturdy clasp—is more pleasurable to wear. As a perennial, it's worth its weight in gold.

GOLD. As man has known since the Incas, gold is loot worth killing for. It is a piece of the sun on earth. He who possesses it is at the life source. The booty of pirates and train robbers, of kings and counterfeiters, gold affords psychological advantage. As currency, it sets a standard against which true value is measured. Symbolically, it is the light of consciousness making order out of elemental chaos. According to the ancient science of alchemy, gold in the laboratory of human nature symbolizes the elemental ego, the untarnishable essence of life. In combination with other alloys, it measures purity and integrity—character. So be aware of how you wear it. Oversized, overstated, or very expensive jewelry can be distracting in a professional setting. The bolder the design, the more panache one needs to carry it off. A sculptural collar has a masculine, alpha-drive quality to it, as if it could be worn by a sun king. Consider all elements in the equation. Gold injects enough glamor to enhance the most monastically simple outfit for a night out or can add understated elegance to everyday wear.

A CHARMED LIFE

CHARM IS THE QUALITY THAT NO WOMAN WANTS TO BE WITHOUT. HENCE THE LASTING APPEAL OF THE CHARM BRACELET—A KIND OF RUSTLING SKIRT FOR THE WRIST. APART FROM

the wedding band, it could be the most sentimentally valued jewelry on earth. A collection of souvenirs strung together and acquired over time, it dangles in view girlhood dreams, rites of passage, adventure, transformative travel, and true love. It charts anniversaries and births in sterling silver or gold and, in so doing, becomes an instant heirloom. Delightfully playful for its tinkling music, the charm bracelet makes a female presence felt—during the blackouts of the London Blitz, women were advised to wear them, like cowbells, in the dark. They have flourished in ultrafeminine times—the Victorian and Edwardian eras, and the fifties. Great keepers of the charm bracelet include the Duchess of Windsor—she was given a jeweled cross by her prince for all her trials—whose life became one long record of a love story. If you start a bracelet, make sure the chain you choose is sturdy enough to hold more charms than you bargained for.

THE DUKE OF GOLD. Fulco Santostefano della Cerda, Duke of Verdura, gave the twentieth century its contemporary relaxed notion of how to wear gold. The jeweler to Dietrich, Garbo, and Chanel, he reinvented the wheel of real jewelry, giving it the fun and fantasy of the fake. He used gold and colored stones with diamonds in fanciful naturalistic and baroque forms.

The more surface intrigue, the better: mix shiny with matte, glitter with a satin finish, transparent plastic with pearls. Combinations of material are limited only by the imagination. The more it shimmers, the dressier it becomes.

Off-white elegance. Pale color has a princely attitude that makes it at once casual and refined. Pale metallics—silver and gold—make a natural match.

A leopard print, however dramatic, is extremely versatile and can appear casual depending on what it's worn with.

ALCHEMY

The idea that silver and gold don't go together is strictly old hat. In fact, if you look into alchemy, the science of the metallurgy of the soul, you'll find that gold is to silver as sun is to moon, as masculine is to feminine, and all of which they symbolize. Celestial harmony, metallurgic magic, cosmic style is in the mix. Just make sure it doesn't look like an accident. Gold and silver are most successfully married when lined up side by side: a gold ring against a silver one. Similarly, contrasting matte and shiny surfaces bring out the drama of each other.

MATTE GOLD CUFF

SILVER CUFF

ACRYLIC CUFF

SIMPLE LESSON gold & silver

INTAGLIO BRACELET
Engraved or carved stones
(*intaglio* derives from the Italian
verb for "engrave") in gemstones,
coral, and crystal were used as
seals by the Greeks.

"Jewelry isn't meant to make you look rich. It's meant to adorn
you. And that's not the same thing."
COCO CHANEL

COLOR

OFTEN ADDING DRAMA TO ACCESSORIES, COLOR CAN BEDAZZLE, WHICH MAY ACCOUNT FOR OUR FASCINATION WITH GEMSTONES. IT IS ENTERTAINMENT AND SURPRISE. THE PUREST, most vibrantly colored stone is generally the most valuable. Semiprecious stones—citrine, peridot, tourmaline, topaz—are increasingly appreciated as "fun" fine jewelry that won't put you in hock. Like their more precious cousins—rubies, emeralds, diamonds—gemstones are natural minerals that possess beauty, relative rarity, and a reasonable degree of durability and value—the technical definition of a gem—but without the cost. The art of imitating gems excelled with the paste of eighteenth-century jewelry. Now the semiprecious stone is likely to be treated like an Etruscan treasure, set in matte gold as a contemporary "heirloom."

GEM DANDY

Color is the determining factor in a gemstone's value—the purest in hue is worth the most. Glass has been the gemstone facsimile of choice since the Egyptians for the way it captures color. **RED:** ruby, garnet, diamond, bloodstone. **GREEN:** emerald, peridot, jade, tourmaline. **BLUE:** sapphire, diamond. **BLACK:** onyx, jet. **YELLOW:** citrine, diamond, zircon, garnet, amber. **BROWN:** smoky quartz, topaz. **WHITE:** pearl, moonstone, jade, chalcedony. **COLORLESS:** zircon, quartz, topaz, moonstone, diamond.

W A T C H E S

EMBLEMS OF EFFICIENCY, WATCHES HAVE ASSUMED INORDINATE STATUS IN WESTERN CULTURE AS signs of social worth—perhaps this is because free time is scarce. Formerly, gentlemen thought it gauche to wear a watch for the way it suggested preoccupation with time. This logic still holds at formal parties, where women wearing watches are considered killjoys. Drop the watch in your

handbag instead of wearing it. Traditionally, watch style observed setting and season: the diver's watch for the beach, the Timex at your desk. But those rules have broken down. If you are likely to run on your lunch hour, the Ironman, Timex's triathlon time-keeper, may be just the thing. President Clinton wore one to his inaugural ball. Your main time-piece should be able to adapt to most of what you do and wear.

AS TIME GOES BY

ROLEX OYSTER WATCH. The Oyster was the world's first waterproof watch, patented in 1926. It mixes silver and gold, which enables it to go with any jewelry and in any locale: uptown or at the beach. **"DESIGN" WATCH.** Adamantly minimalist. **CLASSICS.** The Cartier Tank watch and the Timex Mercury watch, with a round face and flex band, introduced in the fifties and still ticking. **IRONMAN.** The triathlon watch from Timex is the best-selling watch in the country for its high-tech accuracy, water resistance, 8-lap recall, 16-hour stopwatch, three-mode countdown timer, lighted day-and-date display, and alarm. It delivers a sense of adventure.

[🕮 BUYING TIPS *first aid—page 159*]

THE SWATCH

Since 1983, this Swiss watch
company has combined the
smooth timekeeping of Swiss
mechanisms with the fun of the
fabulous plastic fake. Swatch
has made the watch a canvas to
draw on, in limited editions, by
artists from Keith Haring
to Vivienne Westwood.

GOLDFINGER

Rings have the appeal of talismans, things that will keep you safe—from infidelity and fire and brimstone. They speak of moral and sentimental values: they identify the higher powers of pontiffs, kings, and dons. They were used as one's word of honor, a seal and signet certifying provenance. This history of power creates the natural instinct to wear rings in multiples. (Exercise caution in wearing multiples by making sure there is balance and proportion.) On the other hand, one can't ignore the power of a single band of gold.

 BANDS OF GOLD. The triple band ring in three types of gold, created by Louis Cartier in 1924 for the playwright and artist Jean Cocteau, represents a trinity of feelings: friendship (white), fidelity (yellow), and love (pink). Its fluid curve was radical for its day—angular art deco was then the norm. The ring has since been reinvented at Cartier as a trio of interlocked bangle bracelets.

RING-A-DING. Randy Travis: "On the Other Hand." Greg Brown: "This Band of Gold." Wagner: The Ring Cycle. Johnny Cash: "Ring of Fire." Gary Lewis and the Playboys: "This Diamond Ring."

"An unadorned woman is like an exquisite painting without a frame."

SIMON J. CRITCHELL, *President and CEO, Cartier, Inc.*

René Lalique, the master artisan, jeweler, and sculptor of Belle Epoque Paris, understood the ability of glass to charm like a gem. Recently, Lalique's 1931 design of a crystal cabochon ring—a bubble that presaged the organic, happy style of the sixties—has been reissued in fourteen colors. Like the future it suggested, it's relaxed, glamorous, and glossy.

H E A D W A Y

"Her hat—oh, her hat. It was romance, it was mystery, it was strange, sweet sorrow; it was Lily Wynton's hat, of all the world, and no other could dare it. Black it was, and tilted, and a great, soft plume drooped from it to follow her cheek and curl across her throat. Beneath it, her hair had the various hues of neglected brass. But oh, her **hat**."

DOROTHY PARKER, *Glory in the Daytime*

Z O N E   F O U R

- ☐ BLACK-RIMMED SUNGLASSES
- ☐ CASHMERE MUFFLER
- ☐ GOLD NECKLACE
- ☐ ELASTIC HAIR BAND
- ☐ GOLD BRACELET
- ☐ HOOP EARRINGS
- ☐ PEARL OR DIAMOND STUDS
- ☐ PEARL OR GOLD NECKLACE
- ☐ SUN HAT

HEADS UP

ACCESSORIES ABOUT THE HEAD AND NECK FOCUS EYES ON YOU. IMAGINE PAINTING A SELF-PORTRAIT. ACCESSORIES HELP YOU MANIPULATE THE OUTCOME. THEY CAN HELP TO

show off your best features. By repeatedly choosing a piece, it becomes a part of your look, a trademark—think Barbara Bush and her pearls. Or it could be the way you wear your hair—think Whoopi Goldberg and her dreadlocks. Style is a matter of guiding character to the surface through color, line, and proportion. Face

ZONE FOUR
This zone gets attention whether you want it or not. Accessories here have the power to conceal or add sparkle.

shape; distance between the eyes, across the cheekbones, and from chin to collarbone; and shoulder width are the reference points by which to weigh choices. The bolder the angles, the more dramatic the accessories can be. And don't neglect comfort. If your earlobes are in agony, it will show on your face.

HAIR. Headband. Haircut. Hair color. Earrings. Barrette. Hat. Beret. Baseball cap. Sun hat. Bandanna. Ribbon. Bobby pin. Hair comb. Hat pin. Hat band. Kerchief. Hood. Snood. Beanie. Bow. Earmuffs. Ski hat. **EYES.** Eyeglasses. Eye color. Mascara. Eyeshadow. False eyelashes. Contact lenses. Sunglasses. Ski goggles. Horn rims. Reading glasses. **MOUTH.** Lipstick. Lip liner. Lip gloss. **NECK.** Necklace. Choker. Scarf. Beads. Strand of pearls. Chain. Muffler. **EARS:** Hoops. Studs. Clip-ons. Drop earrings.

[HATS *first aid—page 156*]

NECKING

Long necks can carry large beads and chokers. Short necks are enhanced by long necklaces, which create an illusion of length.

PATTERN

Any pattern used in this zone will compete with your facial features. Small-scale prints are easier to carry off.

FRAMED

Use color like makeup: to complement hair and skin tone and to bring out your eyes. Don't be afraid of wearing shades that contrast with your natural coloring.

LE BERET

Central to French style, it is one of the easiest hats to wear—lots of bohemian attitude but remains flexible on all counts. It adapts to almost any hairstyle and packs well.

MONO-A-MONO

Muted color schemes and subtle contrasts are more adaptable than bright colors.

OPPOSITES ATTRACT

Neat studs or clip-on earrings with a chunky necklace. The boyish beret and soft, feminine chiffon scarf are a classic match of opposites.

Don't let accessories in a zone fight each other. Let one be the most commanding in size or design.

The closer a hat clings to function—protecting you from the elements—the less likely it will look foolish on you.

H A T S

EVER SINCE MARY TYLER MOORE TOSSED HER
BERET INTO THE AIR, THE HAT HAS BEEN SOMETHING
THE MODERN WOMAN HAS THROWN OFF, TO HER STYLISTIC

disadvantage. Hats are a blatant style statement, flattering and flirtatious. "The way you wear your hat," as the song goes, can be grounds for undying devotion. Hats signal social ceremony—a day at the races, a wedding—or festivity. They work best as a point of contrast—in color and texture—to clothing. Matching them to clothes could make you look like the Queen of England. Hats have a sense of humor as well as formality: you can look sublime or, if you're not careful, ridiculous. Hats, however, were created to serve a purpose: protection from the sun or providing warmth in the cold. Style follows, whether you're Lara in the snow or Huck Finn on the Mississippi. There is no subduing their impact. They frame the face and allow for bolder makeup. As usual, round faces look best with angular hats, and vice versa.

FREE AGENT

The baseball cap—you've probably taken it from someone, but it's become a trusty friend. Wearing it, you've painted your apartment, walked the dog, played tennis, and gone on vacation.

"A little bad taste is like a nice splash of paprika."

DIANA VREELAND

KNIT CAP

The knit hat is of simple handmade origins dating back to the invention of knitting needles. These hats have been worn the world over by skiers, fishermen, night club ravers, and burglars—a true global vernacular. But no one could ever wear it better than Cary Grant in *To Catch a Thief*.

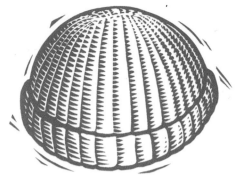

TIBETAN WASHA HAT

The name derives from the Tibetan word for fox (the typical fur used to edge the hat). The crown is often made from colorful silk and ties in the back for a snug fit.

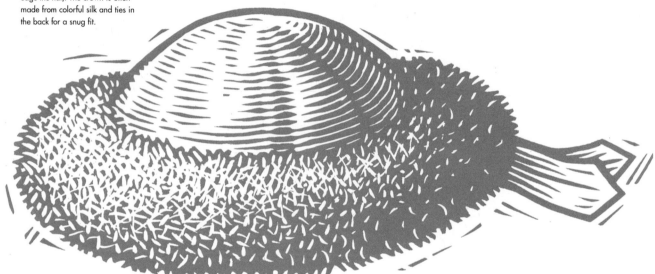

talking **heads**

 Never confuse style with function.

FEDORA

This hat has been a popular unisex classic since the late nineteenth century. Though this felt hat with a soft brim hails from the Austrian Tyrol, its name derives from *Fédora*, a play performed in Paris in 1882.

💡 Ornamental hats shouldn't say more than you can say.

CLOCHE

Because of its shape, this hat goes by the French word for "bell." It first came out in 1915, but was all the rage in the twenties, complementing the newly chic bobbed and permanented hairstyles.

CAP

Originally worn by workmen, this cap has been popular with sporty men since the turn of the century. In the sixties it appeared in flamboyant sizes and colors and was worn by women as well.

INSTANT ELEGANCE

THE COCKTAIL HOUR STRIKES. THE JACKET COMES OFF. A NEW YOU—THE REAL YOU—EMERGES FROM BEHIND YOUR DESK, BOUND FOR DINNER WHEREVER,

and, one hopes, later breakfast at Tiffany's. Delightfully feminine details—a spindly shape, a sparkling surface, a colorful sheen—convert the plainest of sheaths into a sensation. And still the little black dress retains all its legendary decorum. It's the Audrey Hepburn factor, plus the amount of limb that is flashed—arm, neck, knee: nature's own accessories. Such balletic charm inspires prim, pretty punctuation. Alternately, accessories can add the drama, the sweetness, the naughtiness, and the pizzazz.

THE ULTIMATE ACCESSORY

Like the hat, the little black dress focuses all eyes on the face. This most fundamental piece of clothing qualifies as an entire wardrobe when worked over with accessories. It is the accessory to all accessories. Coco Chanel created it in the twenties, and it soon became the antifashion item of the century—it is the one piece of clothing that is, ipso facto, your own. It mimics the uniforms of shop girls and waitresses—anonymous and unadorned. It gave evening clothes the relaxed attitude of tennis dresses. In Chanel's first versions it was matched with a neat, small hat for the cocktail hour. It makes limbs, elbows, neck, and collarbone elements of adornment. The rest is gravy.

CLASSIC. Dark shoes, dark purse, dark glasses, pearls at the ears and neck—all make way for a decorative hat.

RELAXED

Simple for evening: pearls, elegant pumps, a tasteful purse, and a jewel of a buckle.

When dressing sparely, every item counts—like the patent-leather sandal: the bohemian basic gets a downtown tweak.

POLISHED

"She was never without dark glasses, she was always well groomed,

TRUMAN CAPOTE,

LUNCH

DINNER

Nighttime is an opportunity to funk it up. A stylized handbag, a decorative belt, and exaggerated hoops make for a grand entrance.

Sensible chic: the tote that contains everything and shoes for when you're on the go.

there was a consequential good taste in the plainness of her clothes…"

Breakfast at Tiffany's

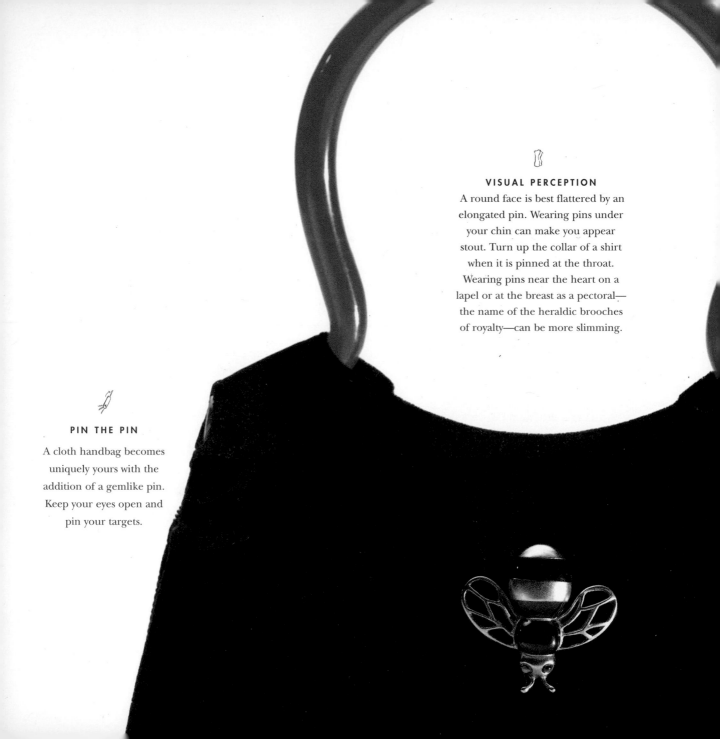

VISUAL PERCEPTION

A round face is best flattered by an
elongated pin. Wearing pins under
your chin can make you appear
stout. Turn up the collar of a shirt
when it is pinned at the throat.
Wearing pins near the heart on a
lapel or at the breast as a pectoral—
the name of the heraldic brooches
of royalty—can be more slimming.

PIN THE PIN

A cloth handbag becomes
uniquely yours with the
addition of a gemlike pin.
Keep your eyes open and
pin your targets.

P I N S

PINS ARE PORTABLE BUTTONS, SMALL WORLDS

OF ORNAMENT THAT GO WHERE YOU WANT THEM TO,

THAT DO YOUR BIDDING AT THE SHOULDER, COLLAR, HAT, OR

waist. Their historic function as suture for untailored garments has been subverted by sheer

playfulness. They are gregarious little items, a bit like name tags for the way they introduce

themselves on your behalf. Stickpin, punk safety pin, kilt pin, circular brooch, or pin-

pendant—each has its own point to make. Great periods for the pin this century include the

forties, when playful plastics put fun into the picture, as well as the early sixties, when

they were matched to necklaces. Unlike the brooch, the little pin main-

tains a certain purposefulness: the hat, hair, and tie pin ornament utility.

TO THE POINT. The red ribbon, the lapel pin designed to raise public awareness of the AIDS crisis, has become the most visible emblem of shared feeling since the peace sign. Designed in 1991 by the fifteen members of the New York group of artists Visual AIDS, the inverted V is like an upended victory medal colored valentine red. It was conceived to be a shared lament or prayer—the kind of thing a lot of people would be willing to wear. As such, it has helped relieve the stigma of the illness by star association. With support from Broadway Cares/Equity Fights Aids, the entertainment industry's AIDS foundation, 3,000 of the pins were made by hand for the 1991 Tony Awards ceremony. It has since appeared at the Emmys, the Grammys, and the Oscars. Ribbons keep turning up to tell a story: a pink one is now worn to show breast-cancer awareness, yellow for prisoners of war.

The Brooch. An important-looking pin, the brooch was part of the nineteenth-century "parure," or set, which included a necklace, a ring, earrings, bracelets, a brooch, and sometimes a head ornament in fine gems. In the hands of the great jewelry designers of the twentieth century, the brooch acquired its own, more design-driven personality. It became sculptural, stylized, and often abstracted from forms in nature, as well as African and Oriental art. Some of the more memorable brooches in recent history have taken the shapes of leaves, articulated flowers (like a jeweled boutonnière), and birds in flight. However sophisticated the wearer, the impulse to adorn oneself with images from nature is primitive, perhaps even innate. They are worn today as they were by the caveman: as a kind of interface with the natural and supernatural worlds, a way of appropriating their power.

MARCASITE

Marcasite is one of the less flashy ways to shine. An iron mineral with a metallic luster, it looks like a dark and smoky mirror or the surface of a bottomless pond. This stone, as hard as quartz, was especially popular in the nineteenth century, when the actress Sarah Bernhardt wore it. The Incas loved it in the sixteenth century; in the seventeenth, it was used to set off fine colored gemstones. Even contemporary marcasite pins and rings set in pavé have the air of estate jewelry. Marcasite charms by being elusive, with a color that is difficult to define—brown to black with yellowish highlights.

THE PIN WARDROBE. Pins fall into lean-lined stickpin shapes—the hat pin, the lapel pin—and the more sprawling brooch, the kind of shape that holds a collar closed. Pins are an opportunity to subtly add personal flair. Crystals indicate mood and mystery. Florals evoke pure femininity. The dress clip works well at the neckline of dresses, as was the fashion in the thirties and forties, when they were worn in pairs. **CLASP.** A decorative pin worn over a clasp can reinvent the simplest of necklaces. **LAPEL PIN.** Signature items. Wear them separately or in clusters. **KILT PIN.** The original safety pin, the kilt pin is handsome not only for Liam Neeson and Mel Gibson. Decorated with crystals, for instance, it becomes a more romantic proposition. **BROOCH.** The important pin, it spreads its wings often in the form of birds and insects.

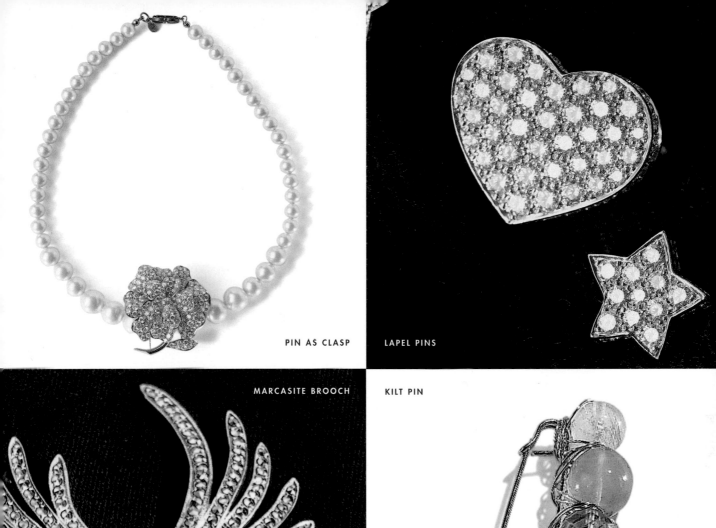

PIN AS CLASP

LAPEL PINS

MARCASITE BROOCH

KILT PIN

FOREVER LINKED IN THE MIND'S EYE WITH BONNETS, BALLERINAS, AND PRETTY GIFT PACKAGES, THE BOW is festive and essentially happy—a good-time accessory. It is also girlish, as

B it can be entirely homemade and slid onto anything—onto a bobby pin or a barrette, around multiple strands of pearls, around the wrist, or worn as a

O pedestal for a pin. Black is its most classic color. Worn at the neck of a

bbons and bows and furbelows, that's what little girls are made of."

innocent as Alice in Wonderland. The French have a knack for using it in a way that suggests feminine sophistica-tion. Chanel liked it as backdrop for her camellia in silk, worn at the neck or wrist. In satin ribbon or grosgrain,

W man's white shirt, with pearls and chains, it has a haunting Victor–Victoria quality. In any incarnation it signifies dress-up. It implies freedom from labor, playful inefficiency. Like

S the tuxedo tie on a penguin suit,

MEMORABLE BOW BEARERS: LITTLE BO PEEP • ELOISE • ALICE IN WONDERLAND • SALLY BOWLES • PEE-WEE HERMAN

HEADBAND

HAIR PIN

SCRUNCHY

ELASTIC BAND

BARRETTE

HAIR

AS LITTLE GIRLS KNOW, THE FACT THAT YOU CAN PLAY WITH BARBIE'S hair is what makes her so compelling. Hair is provocative, subtly sensational. Okay, it's about sex. Flowers in the hair are the instinctive response to the siren call of hairstyling, and since Eve have symbolized virginity and purity and its corollary, deflowering. Keeping this provocation under wraps has been the job of hair ornaments and coverings throughout time. In Western art, only the Virgin Mary, Mary Magdalene, and the Mona Lisa were allowed to appear with tresses loose. Long, untamed hair draws the eye down, while

SCENT
is a personal memento of deep, unconscious provocation. Some choose to wear a single scent for life, like one's name. But scent can also be coordinated to the season or the hour: a fresh citrus scent for summer or day, a musky scent for winter or after dark. A little dab will do you—behind the ear. Settings in which perfume might be inappropriate: job interviews, airplanes, movie theaters.

LIPSTICK
brings color to the face and should complement clothing as well as skin tone and hair. Deep red, referred to as "lipstick red," can put even casual clothes in the mood to step out.

short hair emphasizes the face: it's up to you to decide what you want to accentuate. The debutante headband, the schoolgirl barrette, the cheerleader's elastic band—they all apply a wholesome, castigating restraint to wild manes. This in itself is provocation—to let one's hair down. Witness the major pastime of schoolboys at assembly: pulling girls' hair.

HAIR IMPLANTS?
Without some means of tying hair back, most women would go instantly mad. Choice in ornaments has expanded considerably, each with its own effect. Those in fabric tend to be more girlish. Filigree in metal or tortoiseshell is womanly. René Lalique made them in ivory and enamel during the Belle Epoque. Hair color can be its own accessory: think of Susan Sontag's gray streak.

EARRINGS

THESE BAUBLES THAT ADORN THE EARS ARE THE FOUNDATION OF FEMALE ARMATURE. THEY ARE ANCIENT EMBLEMS OF ROLE-PLAY. WOMEN IN TRIBAL CULTURES HAVE THEIR

ears pierced at puberty to signify that they are essentially "all ears," willing to listen to the higher authority of the male partner. This is a subtext not lost on modern society. Earrings demonstrate attentiveness. Like another pair of eyes, they shed light on a conversation—the face. They have performance value, which makes some women feel undressed without them. All earrings add a sparkle, though each type has its own different attitude: The neat clip-on can be business-like. The dramatic drop is romantic, appropriate to evening. The short drop has demure grace. The stud is sporty and fuss-free. The diamond stud can go from the beach to the ball. The pearl stud, more fragile, can also be sporty or dressy. The notion of matching earrings to a necklace is a mark of neoconservative glamor. On principle, however, they needn't match as long as they have something in common: material, shape, or size should contrast, not fight. What does matter are necklines: bare, open, or V neck look best with long drop earrings.

"If you have a choice of two things and can't decide, take both."
GREGORY CORSO

HOOPTY-DO

IT'S THE BAND OF GOLD THAT CAN BE WORN WITHOUT ANY COMMITMENT, AND STILL IT MAKES A STATEMENT. THE HOOP IS A HAPPY FORM: A CONTINUOUS SMILE.

To wear it is to express a certain *jeunesse d'esprit*. You won't find an old lady—or, at least, one who is old at heart—wearing them. A mere circle, the hoop is at once primitive and modern. It's been with us since well before Sinbad the sailor and Captain Hook. Transcending its piratical origins, it is truly global jewelry, as internationally recognized as the stop sign.

The French wear them Brigitte Bardot style, oversized and swinging from clip-ons, with stiletto heels. The hoop is always sporty, if racy, which is why young men have gotten in on the act. In this simplest of forms, size, shape, and color make all the difference.

DUMBO

Hoop earrings are light if they are hollow; avoid heavy ones that can stretch the earlobe over time.

Surface effects are determining. Reminiscent of boat-shaped hoop earrings of antiquity, this hoop takes a modern turn with Morris's signature 24-karat gold matte finish and organic shape.

ARTWEAR

ROBERT LEE MORRIS. Organic form and timeless symbol are the hallmarks of the designs of Robert Lee Morris, a jeweler who, along with Elsa Peretti, has promoted in America the decorative language of "artwear"—the name of his first boutique—in silver and gold: highly emblematic, timeless pieces that, like the talismans of old, are good for morale as well as a pleasure to touch. This is jewelry that in period and provenance belongs only to the wearer. Famous for his matte finishes, Morris sometimes applies 24-karat gold to a shiny surface of brass beneath, with glowing results.

PEERING INTO THE EYE OF A BRILLIANT-CUT DIAMOND IS LIKE STANDING ON THE EDGE OF A PRECIPICE, OR a dream. Kings wore diamonds as evidence of the divine right

DIAMONDS

of rule. In the Middle Ages, the diamond was thought to reconcile spouses and to keep one out of harm's way. It was worn uniquely by men of royal birth until the first official courtesan of the French court—no, it wasn't Marilyn—made it a girl's best friend. Agnès Sorel boasted the first diamond necklace ever seen on a woman, commissioned for her by her lover, King Charles VII. A diamond still represents security—a piece of the rock, a token of a powerful man's esteem, even if it's your husband's. During turbulent times a diamond is a mobile asset—it withstands revolutions in relationships, politics, or a country's currency A diamond's value is forever.

CUTS

Round (also called brilliant), oval, pear, marquise, emerald, cushion, square.

QUALITY

Determined by a combination of factors: **cut** (quality of craftsmanship), **color** (often, the darker the hue, the more valuable the stone), **clarity** (lack of flaws in the stone), and **carat weight**. Size isn't everything. Blue and red diamonds are available only in small stones; a large yellow diamond is generally worth far less than a tiny red diamond, for instance.

COLORS

Nearly colorless, pink, red, brown, yellow, brownish, yellow, green, blue (the color of the famous Hope diamond), and black.

The Great Impostors. Cubic zirconia. This simulated diamond is so good at what it does that it has fooled even the experts. In Washington, D.C., a "nice couple" shopping for loose, brilliant-cut 1-carat diamonds deftly replaced real stones with CZ at several reputable jewelers before anyone noticed. Not to be confused with zircon, a diamond substitute found in nature, CZ is a man-made imitation that looks like a diamond but with more "fire" and slightly less "brilliance"—jeweler's terms for the way light dances in a faceted stone. Sold since 1974, it is the most durable diamond substitute—others can be soft or brittle and chip and scratch easily. CZ can also be produced in red, green, and yellow. The challenge is knowing what you're buying. If you're shown a sapphire or amethyst ring with "diamonds," ask whether the diamonds are real. CZ is about 75 percent heavier than a diamond of the same "spread," or surface dimension: a CZ that looks like a 1-carat diamond weighs 1¾ carats.

RHINESTONES, called "strasses" by the French, were invented by Josef Strasser from glasslike paste, in the 1750s. Marie Antoinette wore them. The name "rhinestone," it is guessed, comes from the fact that Strasser's homeland was the Rhine river valley in Germany. PASTE a glass composition, has been used since antiquity to imitate gemstones of all colors. Artisanry of this fake jewelry was superb and popular in the eighteenth century, when it was considered "valuable," even if the stones were not real. Paste, often colored deep blue and set in foil, allowed for inventive designs that were impractical to cut in precious stone. Paste became definitively second-rate in the nineteenth century, when it was used exclusively to imitate diamonds.

EYEGLASSES

YOU CAN TELL WHEN A HOLLYWOOD ACTRESS WANTS TO SEEM MORE THAN JUST ANOTHER pretty face: she starts wearing professorial glasses in public, and her perceived IQ jumps several points. Glasses channel interpersonal exchange. They are the frame through which you are received and, as such, easily become a stylistic signature. They always imply intelligence, and often mystery and glamor. Pick a frame according to your purpose and personality. Do you want to appear tough or tender, sophis-

James Dean Harold Lloyd *T. S. Eliot* Jodie Foster *Jean-Paul Sartre*

Groucho Marx *Ernest Hemingway* Theodore Roosevelt *William Hurt* John Lennon *Mahatma Gandhi* Joseph Stalin *Le Corbusier* I. M. Pei

Daryl Hannah *Marlee Matlin* Selma Diamond *Lina Wertmuller*

Roy Orbison *Tom Cruise* Don Johnson *The Blues Brothers* Jack Nicholson

ticated or naive? Glasses reshape the face in flattering, illusionistic ways. Learn to manipulate their magic. Choosing well requires patience and a good selection to sample. Try different frames on, again and again, and compare the effect. The round face can be slimmed by angular cat's-eye glasses, the angular face softened by round frames. The oval face can carry almost any frame. Color and material are key to the overall impression: mottled tortoiseshell and horn-rim–like plastics are warmer in mood than metal.

[🕮 EYEGLASSES *first aid—page 159*]

FRAME SHAPE. The brow line of the frames should follow and cover your own eyebrows to create a look that "fits." A solid, prominent bridge will make the nose look shorter and the eyes appear closer together.

LENSES. Bifocals and trifocals that allow you to see both near and far no longer have to advertise themselves with horizontal lines running across the lenses. "Hidden-line" lenses look like any other but they cost more.

HIGH-TECH, LOW-TECH. What looks like tortoiseshell, horn, or heavy metal creates less of a burden on the nose in new lightweight materials: stainless steel, titanium, graphite, and nylon.

COLOR. Be aware that color attracts attention, particularly if it's darker than your hair color. Choose carefully.

BLACK FRAMES. Existentialism lives. Round black frames made famous by the architect Le Corbusier remain the hallmark of the intellectual. However spare, they conjure up the bohemian glamor of Parisian cafés in the fifties.

THE BIG PICTURE

Sometimes an entire character can be conjured in the choice of frames and the way you wear them. The addition of a pearl eyeglass chain takes its cue from the mother-of-pearl frame, itself a strong statement. Together they have a mock tenderness that on the right woman strikes a pose of youth through old-ladyish metaphor.

Metallica

Cyberchic and sunglasses have a lot
in common. Both deal with the ozone and
bend the mystique of hyperspace to their own stylistic
purpose. It's easy to feel powerful wearing wraparound silver shades. They positively parade personality. They strike the
pose. They give you room to gauge your own responses to the world
from the "dugout" of the dark lens, especially if the lens is mirrored.
As the hole in the ozone layer expands, sunglasses have become good
for your health as well as your attitude: they deliver necessary UV protection throughout the year. Outdoor light can be twenty-five times
brighter than indoors. Sunglasses should block between 15 and 35
percent of available light. Try them on in the store. Look in the
mirror. If you can easily see your eye, the lens is too light.
Wraparound frames fend off sidelong rays, but distor-
tions can sometimes result from curved lenses.
Some $10 glasses are just as effective sun
protection as $100 ones.

TOUJOURS HERMÈS

As an emblem of elegance the Hermès scarf just won't quit, no matter how much it's copied. Originally a luxury saddlery firm, Hermès has been creating scarf patterns since 1937 that incline to equestrian and nature imagery in multicolored silkscreened 36-inch squares. All are hand-rolled; their plush texture is a trade secret.

SERVICE AND STYLE MEET ON THE FORMLESS GROUND OF THE SCARF—ALL TEXTURE, COLOR, PATTERN, AND tactility, with infinite possibilities. This accessory has super powers: it can enhance or camouflage as well as expand your wardrobe by changing the attitude of many outfits. It

QUINTESSENCE

simplifies through reinvention. The scarf is capable of clothing both the home and the body, as an accent or the main event. The ancients wore it with dazzling simplicity. Only in this century has the Western woman fully seized the scarf's genius. It became a flag of liberated movement as corsets fell away. Isadora Duncan, the free-form dancer who died when her long scarf caught in the wheel of an open car in which she was riding, epitomizes its hold on the twentieth-century imagination as something feminine, exotic, untamed. A scarf invariably plays against form, dressing down or up whatever it's worn with. In silk, it can combine luxury and sportiness in one fell swoop. Quality in silk resides at the edges: are they hand-rolled? In cotton, the scarf is altogether casual—like the bandanna, the blue jeans of scarves.

GO WITH THE FLOW. Especially if it's in a silky fabric that grabs attention with shimmer and color, don't fight the scarf's need for center stage. Avoid knotting it in a way that strangles out its natural sweep and movement. Wear earrings that complement without competing. Keep the neckline clear of clutter. If you are petite, avoid wearing large scarves or shawls.

PAREO

The Main Event. The Romantics believed that the square shawl stoked emotion by framing the heart. Its other missions in life depend on fabric and season. In cashmere or wool, the large, 48-inch square is elegant outerwear, an alternative to a coat over a tailored suit in cool weather. In cotton or silk, it can be worn next to the skin: as a short pareo or as a bib halter, with another scarf tied over it as a belt. Wearing a large scarf at the neck and shoulders requires some finesse: aim for a strategic balance of energy and insouciance. A square scarf should never just hang: it should perform. Scarves should be of a proportion that flatters: a too-small scarf will make a large person look larger.

tie me up TIE ME DOWN

PAREO. Traditionally 5 to 7 feet of oblong cotton wrapped around the torso and tied at the waist or chest, the pareo can keep you stylishly decent for an entire island holiday.

WAIST KNOT. Who needs a belt when a scarf is around? The elegance of the cummerbund is branded on this obi-style sash, loosely tied at the waist. In colorful silk, this oblong dresses up the plainest Jane for evening.

SLIP KNOT. The elegant way to wear a muffler is to first double it up, then wrap it around the back of the neck and slip the loose ends through the loop. An equestrian sense of style is instantly established.

> "A woman's skirt should be like a diplomatic conference—long enough to be decent and short enough to hold people's interest."
>
> ANDRÉ FRANÇOIS POCET

PUNCHY PRINT
The beauty of silk is the way it holds
color. A printed silk scarf dominates the
clothing it's worn with. A strong face
can best carry off a strong print.
Beware of overwhelming patterns
if you're fine-featured.

KARMA CAMELLIA
Chanel made the delicate white
camellia the insignia of her fashion
house as a gesture of mourning for
her one true love, Boy Capel. It was
the flower he most often gave her,
and, like her, it was exquisite.

TWO-TONE
Contrast counts, especially the one-two punch of navy and white. A bag makes a statement when its color contrasts with clothes.

BITS OF GOLD
Gold jewelry goes with everything from blue jeans to cocktail dresses.

STRIPES
The peppy pattern of optical illusion, stripes are sporting and optimistic in character. One of the easiest and most effective ways to wear them is in the scarf. Types of stripes: awning (right), candy, pin, chalk.

Pattern Principle. A little goes a long way. The power of pattern is to be respected: only then does it work wonders. It can pump personality into the plainest garments. Pattern is an emotional Morse code. It works like the spots and stripes of animal skins to distinguish species and provide clannish connection. Whether geometric, floral, plaid, or ikat, it serenades the eye with rhyme.

THE BASIC BACKDROP. Navy suit. White T-shirt. Good watch. The simple uniform.

CHAINS. The gold chain has wound its way around necks since Roman times. In the Renaissance, it was doled out as a sign of royal favor. Today, it's one of the first necklaces a woman invests in.

N E C K L A C E S

All necklaces have an element of bestowed honor, like the lei or an award. Because of this, it takes skill to wear them well. The less cluttered the neckline, the more extravagant the necklace can be. The most flattering materials bring light to the face: pearls, gems, crystals, and gold. The neck ring, a rigid collar, is one of the more dramatic, but to wear it well you should have a long neck. The design you choose depends on what you can carry: the roundness of a face is exaggerated by a round choker. You have to experiment with length and line to see what works for you.

NECK RING

A bold necklace should be complemented with bold earrings or studs.

S I L V E R

IT COSTS LESS THAN GOLD, BUT PRICE CANNOT FULLY ACCOUNT FOR THE OUTLAW APPEAL OF SILVER JEWELRY. LIKE MOONLIGHT, IT CASTS AN ENTHRALLING COOLNESS

that allows bikers and cowboys to wear it and still feel undercover. It has the aura of armor, an "anti" attitude that has costumed the existential angst of teens and artists through the century. It is a modern material—not much used in jewelry design until the industrial age. Silver has a Luddite quality. Because it's significantly cheaper than gold, it lends itself to being handcrafted and rode a wave of ethnic chic in the sixties. Beaten, chiseled, rolled, or cast, it goes equally well with colored stones, urban pallor, or the blush of youth.

> ["Abby,' I said. 'It's New York. They have hundred-and-seventy-dollar haircuts and wear black leather belts with sterling silver buckles.'"
> **TAMA JANOWITZ,**
> *"Slaves of New York"*

WHAT MAKES SILVER STERLING? Pure silver is combined with copper to make it the hard yet workable metal known as sterling. The legal standard for sterling in both the United States and Britain is 92.5 percent silver. **THE TARNISHED TRUTH.** Silver does not tarnish through oxidization, as is often thought. Tarnish results from contact with sulfurous fumes or a thin external deposit, such as dust. Tarnish is removed by a liquid that releases the sulfur. **AGE MATTERS.** Depending on one's coloring, silver is generally less flattering to older skin. Gold casts a warmer, more flattering light close to the face.

LEATHER TOTE
One of the more versatile
all-purpose bags around.

DIVER'S WATCH
It would seem that scuba diving has
become a major pastime, judging by
the number of diver's watches on
wrists. The watch conveys that one is
keen on technique, timing, the details
of survival—whether on the job or
underwater.

DOWNTOWN SILVER
It becomes cool and bohemian
when worn with black.

GENDER SHIFT
The operating principle of sex appeal—contrast—is achieved by playing sobriety with delicacy. The masculine pantsuit is a perfect place for prettiness: a long, shiny, multi-strand necklace; high-heeled sandals.

SPOTLIGHT
An iridescent scarf in pewter shimmers like moonlight and transforms a simple pantsuit into a form of black tie. It puts dazzle where it counts most—near the face.

IN THE CLUTCH
A bag's shape defines mood and occasion. Small and hand-held is most feminine.

EXPOSURE
Know where to subtract. Baring one's heels provides instant sex appeal and exoticism, and can put you in the mood to dance.

NIGHT MUSIC

Like a genie out of a bottle, evening glamor pours from a bag, scarf, shoes, jewelry—and presto, instant elegance. The suit you wore to work becomes a different animal when worn with an iridescent scarf and open metallic-mesh shoes.

metallic

SURFACE TRUTH

The muted surface next to the brilliant enhances the charm of both bracelets.

PEARLS

THEY CAN BE FORBIDDINGLY PROPER OR AS DECADENT AS ANCIENT ROME, WHERE THEY WERE THE RAGE. PEARLS ARE THE MOST SPORTING OF GEMS, AND THE EASIEST

to wear. Never seriously ostentatious no matter how many strands are worn at once, they look as good with blue jeans as they do with a ball gown. Unlike faceted gems, they flatter less-than-perfect skin. Real or cultured, pearls are mysteriously organic—they must be worn in order to keep their luster and are damaged by

> "Your bosom can be fake, your smile can be fake, and your hair color can be fake. But your pearls and your silver must always be real."
> **SOUTH CAROLINA GRANDMOTHER**

perfume. Excellent fakes are worth more than inferior cultured pearls. They can be made with beads of opalescent glass covered with fish-scale extract or a similar luster-creating material. If you are investing in one strand of pearls, go for a convertible style that drops to different lengths via a free-floating clasp.

CHUTE. Single strand. **BAYADERE.** Multiple strands of seed pearls, twisted. **SAUTOI.** Long strand that adjusts in length via a small attachment. **QUALITY.** In a necklace of good quality, pearls match in color and "orient" (light from within) and are well graduated. Pearls should be strung with knots between them in case the strand ever breaks.

FAUX REAL

IT'S A CRUEL, CRUEL WORLD. THERE WILL ALWAYS BE TWO KINDS OF TEMPTATIONS—THINGS YOU WANT AND THINGS YOU NEED. MAKING THEM MATCH UP, MORE OR LESS, IS THE

trick of style. Therein lies value. So, who needs jewelry? Everyone, for reasons ineffable since the dawn of time. From this fundamental foible of human nature, the inspired "fake" has evolved, an invention that has tempted even the most wealthy women of the century. The only way to wear costume jewelry is with supreme confidence. Jacqueline Kennedy Onassis famously wore faux-diamond flower ear clips; Diana, Princess of Wales, faux society pearl chokers. Both items were purchased from Kenneth Jay Lane, the man who hooked high society on the masterful fake: Barbara Bush's triple-strand choker of pearls were also Lane's. Only the enlightened eras of social history (the eighteenth and twentieth centuries) have allowed themselves to have fun with the fake. The Victorians and Elizabethans tended to measure social worth by the amount of real gold one was draped in—a criterion that contributed to the lugubriousness of the age.

 KENNETH JAY LANE. Liz Taylor, Audrey Hepburn, and the Duchess of Windsor have all been his fans. But costume jewelry designer Kenneth Jay Lane cannot top the assignment given him by Jacqueline Onassis to copy a necklace given to her by Aristotle Onassis. Lane's "original" designs for the jet set of the sixties are collector's items, installed in the Smithsonian. Today, his designs sell around the world, as well as on QVC.

CROWN JEWELS. The famous copy Kenneth Jay Lane made, at Jackie O's request, of the necklace given to her by Aristotle Onassis.

"IVORY" NECKLACE

"TORTOISE" BELT

THE IDEA OF USING IVORY AND TORTOISESHELL AS ORNAMENT DATES FROM the beginning of civilization. Ivory was perhaps the prototype of all jewelry. Cave women tended to wear a single tusk on a necklace, like Diana Vreeland did later. The Victorians liked their ivory bracelets carved or inlaid

RAREFIED

into jet. Tortoiseshell was worn by the Romans and has been inlaid through the ages with gold, silver, or mother-of-pearl in combs and brooches. With biodiversity and preservation of endangered species hanging in the balance, quality substitutes for elephant tusk, whalebone, and turtle shell have changed the way we think about these materials. The Convention on International Trade in Endangered Species (CITES) upholds the ban on importing and exporting materials from plants and animals on the verge of extinction. Plastic and other imitations are more acceptable (and less fragile) to wear than the real thing. True ivory in its most beautiful, glossy, and easy-to-work form came from elephant tusks. Ivory also came from the tusk of the hippopotamus and the horn of the narwhal, once believed to be that of the unicorn. Along with bone, celluloid (a plastic) has been a leading ivory imitator, sometimes called "French ivory." Lately, vegetable ivory—such as corozo nut, the seeds of "ivory" palm trees native to South America—has met the demand and is often used for buttons.

TRAVELER'S WARNING. If you buy antique jewelry abroad made from any species that is now protected, you must get official documentation in the country of origin to confirm that the merchandise is over one hundred years old before bringing it into the U.S.

The animal-print scarf provides the right dash of sass against monochromatic clothes.

A beret is jaunty when worn for pleasure as opposed to warmth.

ANIMAL BEHAVIOR

What a little bit of wild pattern will do for a classic shape. Indeed, the more ladylike the form, the better it takes to the *sauvage* sophistication of the animal print—a pattern that has always signaled sensuality, the wild side within. Even the baby ballerina flat becomes sexy under its influence.

FAUX TORTOISE
BRACELET

LEOPARD-PATTERNED
GLOVES

FAUX LEOPARD
BALLET FLATS

SPOTTED
FUR BOOTS

FAUX COWHIDE
SATCHEL

FAUX LEOPARD-FUR BELT

LEOPARD-PATTERNED
SCARF

N E T W O R T H

When does expense become investment? Take a lesson from the stock market: only in the long run. The more use you can get out of the luxury handbag, year after year, the more it warrants the initial high price-tag. But from the start, it has to be what you love, in shape, texture, and proportion; it must work with your wardrobe and lifestyle.

SIMPLE EVENING. Black silk pumps, black evening bag. Diamonds or cubic zirconia

LEATHER TOTE
A large leather tote can be a portable office housing all your essentials: the mobile phone, the laptop, your family photos, your favorite glossy magazines, clear nail polish for the stocking run errant, etc.

A classic silk scarf can soften a conservative business suit.

GOLD BRACELET
A simple link bracelet or necklace adds a touch of metallic shimmer to any ensemble, businesslike or not.

A business agenda bound in leather becomes an accessory even if not worn—it's an extension of your personal style.

PEARL STUDS
Pearl studs can go from boardroom to ball; even glass fakes can have beautiful luster.

FIRST AID

So now you have all the baubles you could possibly desire, but how to keep them looking new? Where to stash those extra pairs of shoes? Which earrings are the least likely to infect your ears? How to salvage a straw sun hat from an afternoon in the rain? What you should know about quality control so you don't get duped. This information can help.

Shoes

SHOP TALK

ESPADRILLE: A flat shoe with a cloth upper and rope sole.

LAST: Shoes are formed around a form of wood or metal called a last; also refers to the final shape of the shoe.

LUG SOLE: Soles with rubber cleats or ridges for added traction.

MULE: A backless shoe, usually an evening slipper; basically a more elegant version of the clog. Characteristically ladylike; connotes lounging in a boudoir.

NUBUCK: Typically made from cowhide through a process that abrades the hide's outer grain to make it mimic the look and feel of buckskin. It tends to feel rougher than suede.

ORTHOTICS: Any device that helps correct, support, and relieve skeletal problems in the feet. Commonly used to refer to specially designed inner soles for the shoes of those suffering from chronic foot pain.

OXFORD: A flat shoe that laces up the front.

PADDOCK: Named after the fenced-in enclosure for animals, and worn for recreational riding, the paddock boot laces up to provide adjustable ankle support. It works with breeches, jeans, or jodhpurs. Less expensive than the dress boot, it's the preferred choice for young riders with growing feet. The sole of the authentic riding boot is always sewn, never glued or bonded.

PUMPS: Perhaps derived from the word "pomp," this refers to the classic dress shoe women wear both day and evening. It exposes the instep and usually has a heel. (The male version of the pump is more like a ballet slipper with a heftier sole and is worn only with formal evening attire.)

SPECTATOR: Any two-toned shoe; the style first became popular in the twenties but has had many revivals since.

THONG: Minimal sandals with a leather or rubber thong attaching the sole to the foot.

VAMP: The toe box of the shoe, covering the toes and instep.

VIBRAM SOLE: Lightweight rubbery sole that adds spring and slip resistance.

WELLINGTON: Classic rubber boot, originating in Britain.

WELT: Extra pieces of fabric or leather that reinforce seams. A welt on a shoe is usually an extra piece of leather between the upper and the sole.

BUYING TIPS. Smooth, even, and close stitching throughout. A soft lining with inverted seams. A smooth insole. No traces of glue. Bends freely when flexed, then resumes shape. **Athletic shoes** should be bought with a particular sport in mind—tennis requires more support for lateral movement, while running demands more heel cushioning. Studies have found that high-top aerobic and basketball shoes don't offer superior ankle support; supportive cushioning is more important. Look for uppers made out of breathable material. For safety, replace shoes as soon as they begin to wear down. **Exotic skins** (such as lizard, ostrich, and alligator) are many times more durable than leather; reptile skins can be ten times tougher. **Oiled natural finishes** may nick and scratch, but they are more durable than polished finishes and ideal for work boots. **Patent leather** resists dirt but can easily dry out and crack. **Polished leather** is the most practical material for dress shoes; it resists dirt, and a good polishing job can compensate for a lot of minor scratches. **Suede** is more vulnerable than leather. Suede soils easily; don't get caught in the rain. Avoid wearing suede outside when salt or sand has been applied to streets and roads—they can stain suede.

FIT. Feet never shrink, so don't buy tight shoes. Lined shoes are even less likely to give than unlined ones. Buy shoes at the end of the day, when your feet have naturally swelled to their full size (which can be up to a 10-percent increase). Also keep in mind that feet can widen with age, during pregnancy, and from inactivity (sitting on a plane or at a desk). **Try them on:** Most of us have feet that vary slightly in width or length. There should be a thumb's width between the end of the shoe and the longest toe. • Be sure that you're trying on shoes with the kind of socks or stockings you'll be wearing with them. • Heels should fit snugly. If your heels are narrow, affix a heel liner.

MAINTENANCE. Leather breathes and needs a day or two after being worn to dry out. The same shoes should not be worn day after day if you want them to last. Polishing leather helps to keep it from cracking; shoe trees maintain shape. Disposable inner soles cushion each step and absorb odor and sweat. Reheel and resole when necessary. Avoid wearing down heels by having taps placed on them immediately after buying (this costs a lot less than having to fix the heels later). **Canvas sneakers (low-tech).** Machine wash in warm water—mild soap, no bleach. • Sneakers will be protected in the spin cycle if washed with a towel. • For best results, place in the dryer immediately after washing. • Machine dry for approximately 45 minutes on highest heat setting. **Espadrilles.** Apply an appropriate protective fabric spray. Spot-clean canvas with mild detergent. Stuff with paper towels to dry. Espadrilles are generally considered to be disposable shoes (if you get caught in the rain, the glue-and-rope soles will be ruined), so they aren't worth investing a lot of money in. **Patent leather.** Wipe clean with a soft cloth. Use shoe products made specifically for patent leather to prevent cracking. **Polished leather.** To polish: 1. Place shoes on a sheet of newspaper. Brush off surface dirt with a rag, paper towel, or soft brush. 2. With a piece of paper towel, apply a thin layer of cream polish in the appropriate color or neutral. Use circular strokes, rubbing in the polish as you go. Do not leave an excessive amount on the surface. 3. When polish is dry, buff with a brush or clean cloth. 4. If not satisfied, repeat the last two steps. In between shoe shines you can buff with a soft cloth. If there is a grease stain on polished leather, first blot with a dry cloth; if the stain remains, try lifting it with a little vinegar. **Suede.** Apply silicone weatherproofing spray before wearing suede shoes for the first time; the spray can trap dirt once it's present on the shoe. Respray several times a season with non-silicone spray (if you wear the shoes frequently). If a "bald" spot develops on shoes, use a very fine grade (00) sandpaper gently on area until the nap lifts. You can also lift the nap by holding shoes over a boiling kettle and brushing them gently with a toothbrush. **Western boots.** Use saddle soap according to directions. Allow to dry a full day between wearings. **STORAGE.** Store with a shoe tree or pack with tissue, to preserve the shape as they dry after wearing. Never store near a heat source because it will dry out the leather. Leather can mildew; store in a dry, ventilated place. Consider storing: In shoe caddies. • Stacked inside their boxes with a packet of salt to absorb moisture and a photo of shoes or label taped to box for easy access. • On shoe racks placed on shelves or floor. • In shoe bags. • In clear plastic boxes with holes punched for ventilation. • In unexpected places that are little used. Noncooks can take advantage of empty kitchen cabinets • The bottom of a garment bag with coordinating dress or suit. • Sandals in baskets. • Thongs with beach equipment in a canvas duffel. • In wire-mesh drawers. • Hang athletic shoes from their laces on hooks inside a door. • Put slippers under your side of the bed. • In flannel, cotton, or any other breathable-fabric shoe bags hung from hooks.

HEALTH. Elevated heels should be worn judiciously as they can cause foot, calf, hip, and back pain. If you plan on wearing heels often: Vary heel heights throughout the day—i.e., wear flatter shoes for commuting. Consider putting padded inner soles in shoes, especially under the balls of the feet. (Thin models are available for dress shoes.) The cushioning will help prevent the foot from sliding forward in the shoe and cramping toes painfully. From a medical standpoint, the safest heel height is one inch or less. Beware of ankle injuries while wearing platforms. *Expert consulted: Suzanne M. Levine, D.P.M., Clinical Podiatric Instructor, New York Hospital–Cornell Medical School.*

Hats

BUYING TIPS. Think size and shape when buying a sun hat—it should protect your head and face from harmful rays (a four-inch brim should be ample). Straw hats should be somewhat resilient; if the straw is so stiff that it threatens to crack when handled, don't buy it. • Linings are not necessary for a quality hat. Though pretty, linings add weight, bulk, and heat, which may be uncomfortable, particularly for summer hats. • Head-size ribbons (what lines the interior crown of a hat) anchor trimmings and help keep the hat securely on the head; 1¼ inches is a good width. • The best hats for travel are unstructured and of fabric: berets, knitted or crocheted hats, baseball hats, etc. • When buying a winter hat, make sure that it covers the ears.

FIT. Measure your head around its widest point, where the hat crown rests: above the eyebrows, and slightly sloping down in the back of the head. Women's hat sizes are often given in inches. The average head circumference is 22½ inches.

MAINTENANCE. Always follow any cleaning instructions that may come with the hat. To clean head-size ribbon, gently wash with a toothbrush using soap and water. Use caution before putting any hat in the washing machine—even if the hat is a floppy style and made of cotton twill, there may be a stiffening product in the brim that makes it not washable. For **cotton** hats it's safer to hand wash with a wet cloth. Stuff wet hat with tissue and allow to air dry. To remove lint and dust from a **felt hat**, gently lay pieces of Scotch tape on the area to be cleaned and immediately lift off. For high-nap velours, lightly brush in the direction of the felt with a nail brush. For **knit hats**, hand wash with a mild detergent in cool to lukewarm water. Lay hat in its proper shape flat on a towel and allow to air dry. **Leather hats** can be sprayed with the same suede waterproofing products used on shoes and jackets. **Straw hats,** especially those with trimmings, shouldn't get wet. To save a straw hat that got wet, stuff with tissue before it dries. If the hat is misshapen when it's dry, try steaming and remodeling by hand, or take it to a hat renovator (sometimes the manufacturer can repair the hat for you). Since most straws are very fine and made from imported materials, finding someone to reweave a straw hat is difficult. If the style allows, try disguising damage with more trimmings. To spruce up **trimmings** on a hat, brush lightly with a soft paintbrush to remove dust. Steam can often revive ribbons or fabric trimmings.

STORAGE. To store, stuff crown and any large bows with tissue and loosely wrap hat in plastic (old dry-cleaner bags work well), being careful not to crush the brim. Then place in a hat box. Hat racks and hooks are not recommended because they can stretch a hat out of shape and allow it to get dusty. *Consultant: Brenda Lynn, Milliner, New York.*

Bags

BUYING TIPS. Will you be carrying a lot of heavy things? Then be sure to buy a bag or backpack that distributes weight evenly across your back, rather than hanging solely from one shoulder. • Backpack as luggage: a waist strap keeps the pack from swinging; a sternum strap reduces the weight on the shoulders; fit should be narrow. • Think function: look for versatile bags that are easily convertible from top-handle to shoulder-strap. For daily use in cities, bags should zip shut.

MAINTENANCE. Avoid overstuffing handbags with heavy objects, which could distort the bag's shape.

Belts

FIT. Buy so that you can close the belt with at least a finger's thickness between tucked-in shirt and belt.

MAINTENANCE. Clean and apply protective spray to canvas, leather, and suede as you would to shoes. Never use colored polish on smooth leather belts and handbags, as it could stain clothing; instead, use neutral-colored cream polishes. • Don't wear your belt too tight; it may deform the shape of the belt and enlarge the holes.

STORAGE. Do not store belts in clothing or belt loops, as this can damage the fabric or shape of a garment. The best way to keep a leather belt's shape is to hang it from its buckle—on a mounted rack, hanger-shaped rack, or hook.

Jewelry

SHOP TALK

BIB: Necklace composed of three or more graduated strands; length may vary.

BRIOLETTE: Usually a diamond, but may also be another transparent gemstone, which is drop shaped and cut to be a longer version of the double-rose cut.

CARAT: Unit of weight for precious stones, equivalent to 200 miligrams. Also see "karat."

DOG COLLAR: Widely known as *collier de chien*. A multistrand necklace clasped tightly around the neck. Great for concealing neck wrinkles.

GEMSTONE: Any crystalline formation can manifest the qualities of a gemstone. The most common gemstones are diamonds, rubies, sapphires, and emeralds.

GOLD ALLOY: A mixture of gold and other metals, usually silver, copper, zinc, or nickel; this combination alters color and hardness.

GRADUATED: Strand composed of beads that gradually increase in size; the largest bead is at the center of the strand, and the smallest bead is at the clasp.

HALLMARK: The first hallmarks were so called because they were instituted by the Goldsmith's Hall in London, which has overseen gold marking since 1300. A hallmark is stamped on gold, silver, or platinum objects to indicate their quality, origin, and maker.

KARAT: Unit for measuring the fineness of gold; one karat represents 1/24 part pure gold in an alloy. Also see "carat."

LARIAT: Necklace over 36 inches long that doesn't connect at the ends.

NACRE: The iridescent crystalline substance that mollusks produce to coat irritant grains of sand, thus creating a pearl.

PRECIOUS/SEMIPRECIOUS: The Federal Trade Commission is considering eliminating the distinction between precious and semiprecious stones, since they are both gems. As it stands, precious gems are cut for overall high quality, while semiprecious gems are generally commercial grade.

OTHER INFORMATION

STORAGE. Rings, necklaces, and bracelets can be stored in a divider tray that separates pieces by category. Necklaces can be hung on decorative hooks or from a custom-designed closet rod. • Small items can be stored in their original boxes in a shallow drawer. • Hang jewelry from pushpins on a bulletin board. • Hang pierced earrings on a piece of framed screening. A clear plastic tackle box helps facilitate finding jewelry.

HEALTH. Some health pointers to keep in mind: Nickel provokes allergic reactions in many people. Be careful when buying earrings that flaunt their "surgical steel posts" because the rest of the earring may be painted or made out of a metal that has the potential of causing infections. Those who are especially allergy prone may consider having the posts, backs, and fronts of favorite earrings electroplated with 24-karat gold to prevent dermatitis. • If you consistently wear heavy earrings, the pierced hole and the lobe may become elongated over time—not a health threat, but many women consider it unattractive. A plastic surgeon can fix both of these problems. It usually involves a 45-minute procedure under local anesthesia in a plastic surgeon's office. Sutures will remain for around seven days, and there should be no scarring. Ears can be repierced three months later, provided there are no complications. • If you want to have big bold earrings without the weight, you can wear hollow hoop earrings. Thin hoops are more prone to getting dented or deformed. • Thirty to 50 percent of people with pierced earlobes suffer from infection, ranging from short-term irritation to keloids (raised scars); therefore, multiple holes multiply the risk. Piercing the ear's cartilage has an even higher complication rate and can be a lot more serious. • Any earring style that exposes the hole to air (such as a dangling wire or small stud) is less likely to cause infection. • Who shouldn't have their ears pierced for health reasons: those whose immune systems are compromised, those with a chronic illness, and those with blood-clotting problems (hemophiliacs and anyone taking anticoagulant drugs). *Expert consulted: Lloyd Hoffman, M.D., Chief, Division of Plastic Surgery, New York Hospital–Cornell Medical Center.*

Gold

BUYING TIPS. The purer the gold, the more expensive it is. Pure gold is 24 karat and is considered too soft to be used for jewelry. The minimum legal karatage in the United States is 10K, or 10/24 pure gold (41.6%). The higher the gold content, the more yellow the color will be. Gold that is mixed with other metals can take on a variety of colors. **Blue gold** is a gold alloy made with iron or arsenic. **Gray gold** contains iron. **Green gold** is made with silver, copper, zinc, and/or cadmium. **Red or pink gold** is an alloy of gold and copper, and may also include silver. **White gold** contains a high percentage of silver (and also, often, nickel, palladium, zinc, and copper) yet is unlikely to tarnish; before the advent of platinum, it was often used as a setting for diamonds. The most commonly used type of gold, **yellow gold,** is an alloy of gold, silver, and copper.

PRICING. Along with weight, take into consideration the design and construction of the piece, the amount of labor it required, and finishing touches such as engraving and polishing.

AUTHENTICITY. Purchasing gold from a reputable jeweler should protect you from underkarating—the practice of marking gold jewelry as having a higher gold content than it actually contains. One way to assure authenticity is only to buy gold that has been stamped with the karat mark by the manufacturer, since the manufacturer can be traced and therefore is obliged to represent the quality of the gold accurately.

Silver

BUYING TIPS. Silver is often combined with copper to increase its hardness. **Sterling silver** in both the United States and Great Britain is required to be 92.5 percent silver and 7.5 percent copper. **Silver plating** is required by law to comprise a certain percentage of the total metal weight; **Silver electroplating** means that a layer only a few millionths of an inch thick has been applied by a chemical process to a nonprecious base metal.

Diamonds

BUYING TIPS. The value of a diamond is determined by its size, its color, the presence of flaws, and the quality of its cut. • Look at unmounted stones against a white background to gauge their color. • Request that all information about the stone, such as carat weight, color and flaw grades, cut, and dimension, be included on the receipt. • Look for large, cloudy areas that diminish the brilliance of the diamond. Large cracks also indicate a more fragile diamond.

Pearls

BUYING TIPS. To determine authenticity, gently rub the pearls against your teeth. If they are real, they will feel slightly gritty, rather than smooth like faux pearls. • Most pearls sold today are cultivated, formed when an irritant is artificially introduced into a mollusk so that layers of a protective pearly nacre will be secreted around it. Pearls can be round or irregular in shape (baroque). Cultured saltwater pearls range in color from pinkish-white to yellow and gray, depending on the oysters and waters they develop in. Cultured freshwater pearls are baroque in shape and a dull milky white. Both can be dyed. Quality in cultured pearls is determined by lustre, surface brilliance combined with a deep glow, surface cleanliness, shape, color, and size.

MAINTENANCE. Silk thread is most often used for stringing pearls, whenever knotting between each bead is necessary. Nylon thread, which is extremely durable and comes in a variety of weights, may also be used. • Frequent restringing is encouraged for maintenance of pearls. • Pearls are mysteriously organic: they must be worn in order to keep their lustre and are damaged by perfume.

Eyeglasses

BUYING TIPS. There are three kinds of ultraviolet rays: harmless UVC rays; UVB, the sunburn rays that can irritate the cornea; and UVA, which, over the long term, can cause cataracts. In large amounts, infrared rays, the sun's heat rays, can cause retinal burns. When shopping for **UVA protection,** keep in mind that sunglasses should transmit only 15 to 35 percent of available light to the eye. Test them in the store by trying them on and looking at your eyes in a mirror: if you can see your eyes through the lenses, the lenses are probably too light. Photochromic lenses would be an exception to this rule, as they lighten and darken with exposure to the sun. **Lens color** determines how they filter out light. **Gray** prevents distortion; colors remain true. **Green** enhances acuity of vision and allows high levels of green-yellow light through to the eye—the light to which the eye is most responsive. **Brown and brown amber** absorb blue light, which is refracted in the air on hazy days; they improve contrast and reduce glare. There are several different **lens types.** **Constant-density lenses** are designed for bright sunshine and glare. **Photochromic lenses** lighten or darken according to the amount of sunlight, and are suited to a variety of conditions. **All-weather photochromic lenses** are for sport. On hazy days they shift from gray to amber to improve contrast and detail. **Mirror lenses** provide glare protection for water or snow sports. **Polarizing lenses** eliminate direct and reflected glare and are good for driving. Check all lenses for surface distortion: they should be perfectly smooth.

MAINTENANCE. Cleaning how-to: **1.** Hold the glasses by the bridge. **2.** Carefully wipe the lenses with warm water and soap (glass cleaner can damage the frame), then rinse. **3.** Dry with a tissue or soft cloth. • Glasses are easily scratched when dry. If you can't use soap and water to clean them, a specially treated lens cloth, such as Luminex, is recommended.

Watches

BUYING TIPS. Practically all standard watches made today use quartz crystals to regulate their time. Quartz watches are the most reliable, since the quartz crystal vibrates at a consistent, known number of cycles per second. Electrical watches are very similar to mechanical watches, except that a battery is regulating a wheel rather than a windup fixture.

"You can always tell what kind of a person a man really thinks you are by the earrings he gives you."

AUDREY HEPBURN, *in "Breakfast at Tiffany's"*

WARDROBE

Throughout the book we have identified pieces that are essential for any wardrobe. Below are lists we've created for you to consider when choosing accessories for various occasions and seasons.

It's up to you to decide what is appropriate for your own wardrobe, lifestyle, and personal style.

BASIC GEAR

- [ ] everyday leather shoes
- [ ] socks, stockings
- [ ] everyday leather or nylon bag
- [ ] all-purpose watch
- [ ] glasses: sunglasses for sun, prescription if needed
- [ ] leather belt

ORNAMENTATION

- [ ] diamond or gold studs
- [ ] gold hoop earrings
- [ ] gold necklace
- [ ] pearl necklace
- [ ] gold bracelet
- [ ] silk scarf
- [ ] hair ornament: elastic, headband, scrunchy
- [ ] manicure: neutral nail color is low maintenance and goes with everything
- [ ] lipstick
- [ ] perfume

INSTANT WORK

Accessories need to be versatile: start with neutral colors, black (can be casual or formal), or brown (more sporty than black). The better the quality, often the better the first impression; also, quality usually lasts longer.

- [ ] work shoes: leather loafers, pumps, ballet slippers
- [ ] neutral stockings: sheer is dressier and more conservative than opaque
- [ ] bag: a leather or nylon tote large enough to hold papers plus laptop
- [ ] a smaller bag within the tote to hold personal items, easy to carry to lunch or if going out after work
- [ ] watch: black or brown leather strap
- [ ] earrings: gold, pearl, or diamond studs or clip-ons
- [ ] gold or pearl necklace
- [ ] gold chain or bangle bracelet
- [ ] neutral nail color
- [ ] subtle makeup

- [ ] subtle perfume
- [ ] silk scarf
- [ ] ornament to tame hair
- [ ] leather agenda
- [ ] pen: Uni-ball or fountain
- [ ] umbrella—black goes everywhere

INSTANT EVENING

Occasions for evening wear run the gamut from cocktails after work to black-tie events to home entertaining (casual yet festive.) Basic evening accessories will always work, but there is room for expansion.

EVENING SHOE BASICS:
- [ ] simple black pumps in satin or silk faille (the thinner and higher the heel, the dressier)

EVENING SHOE EXTRAS:
- [ ] dazzling colors and metallics
- [ ] luxurious textures—velvet in winter, patent in summer
- [ ] prints (animal prints are classic)
- [ ] interesting shapes—bare and strappy in summer

EVENING HOSIERY:

- [ ] sheer black or nude; shimmery sheen optional

EVENING JEWELRY BASICS (DIAMONDS OR PEARLS):

- [ ] studs or clip-on earrings
- [ ] necklace
- [ ] bracelet
- [ ] pins

Any of the above jewelry will work for all evening events, and the simpler the design, the more likely it will also work for day.

EVENING JEWELRY EXTRAS (DRESSES UP THE SIMPLEST CLOTHES):

- [ ] rhinestones
- [ ] boldly shaped gold or silver
- [ ] colorful gemstones
- [ ] black jet, crystals, black pearls
- [ ] large colorful plastics for summer
- [ ] dress up a simple necklace with a dramatic pin to cover the clasp
- [ ] long necklaces
- [ ] necklaces, bracelets, or rings worn in multiples
- [ ] cuff bracelets
- [ ] a velvet bow or a silk flower at the wrist is supremely feminine

EVENING PURSE BASIC:

- [ ] small, black, in silk or satin—avoid hardware, as it will limit its versatility

EVENING PURSE EXTRAS:

- [ ] interesting or bright colors
- [ ] decorative patterns in luxury fabrics or textures
- [ ] jeweled clasp, minaudière
- [ ] velvet in winter
- [ ] dress up an evening bag with a decorative pin

Because the lighting is usually dimmer at evening events, wear slightly more makeup than in daytime, and emphasize either the eyes or the lips—both would be overkill.

EVENING MAKEUP BASIC:

- [ ] red lipstick—for quick dress-up, unless it clashes with your outfit

EVENING MAKEUP EXTRA:

- [ ] red nail polish (fingers and toes)

EVENING FRAGRANCE:

- [ ] if you don't wear it during the day, you will feel dressier with it on at night
- [ ] if you wear a light scent each day, use a more heady or exotic one for evening

EVENING HAIR ORNAMENTS:

- [ ] bows
- [ ] flowers
- [ ] rhinestones
- [ ] shimmery, luxurious fabrics

Simple clothes—especially in black, white, or red—can become dazzling for night with the addition of a sweeping scarf. Large is dramatic, and can serve as a wrap. Oblong can simply drape around the neck.

EVENING SCARVES:

- [ ] shimmery textures—beads, pearls, sequins, velvet insets
- [ ] dressy fabrics—velvets, organza, satin, shantung, silks, chiffon
- [ ] luxurious colors—silver, gold, copper; brilliant blues, magentas, reds
- [ ] interesting prints—animal

A decorative belt may be all you need to dress up the simplest of clothes for evening. It can replace the statement that jewelry often makes.

BELTS:

- [ ] rhinestone or decorative buckle
- [ ] a shiny color—gold or silver leather
- [ ] a metal—gold chain belt, faux gems

INSTANT SUMMER

- [ ] big gold hoop earrings or diamond studs—both wear well at the beach
- [ ] water-resistant watch
- [ ] sun hat
- [ ] sunglasses—check the UV rating
- [ ] summer tote—canvas, straw, or nylon
- [ ] lipstick—gloss or summer color, pinks, frosted colors
- [ ] fragrance: light; try citrus

SUMMER SHOES:

- [ ] leather day sandals
- [ ] beach shoes—espadrilles or rubber thongs
- [ ] sneakers
- [ ] evening sandals—high-heeled and strappy

SUMMER EXTRAS:

- [ ] jewelry in colorful, cheap plastics
- [ ] colorful ballet slippers

INSTANT WINTER

- [ ] sunglasses—weather protection
- [ ] hat
- [ ] gloves
- [ ] muffler—cashmere is softest and looks great day or night
- [ ] sturdy shoes
- [ ] foul-weather boots
- [ ] leather or nylon bag—big enough to protect stuff in inclement weather
- [ ] tights
- [ ] wool socks
- [ ] lip protection—lipstick, gloss

WHERE

So where do you go from here? The options are practically endless. Check out a few fashion magazines to see what's around. Order some catalogues. Still searching? Throw on a pair of shoes and head out to the nearest shop or mall. The following information may help.

FREEDOM OF CHOICE

ADIDAS
800/448-1796
(Sneakers)

AGATHA
800/AGATHA-7 *(Faux jewelry and accessories)*

ANN TAYLOR
800/999-4554 for stores
(Designer clothing and accessories)

ARMANI A/X
212/570-1122
(Giorgio Armani denims and basics)

BANANA REPUBLIC
212/446-3995
(Sportswear and accessories)

BARNEYS NEW YORK
800/777-0087
(Upscale specialty store; carries Bernard Figueroa, Kazuko jewelry, Manolo Blahnik, Miriam Haskell, and Prada)

BASS
800/777-1790
(Weejuns and other classic shoes)

BELGIAN SHOES
212/755-7372
(This is the only place to buy them)

BEN-AMUN
212/944-6480
(Belts, scarves, and jewelry)

BENETTON
800/535-4491
(Casualwear)

BIRKENSTOCK
800/487-9255
(Shoes)

BLOOMINGDALE'S
800/777-4999
(Upscale department store)

BOTTEGA VENETA
800/662-5020
(Leather shoes and accessories)

BROOKS BROTHERS
800/274-1815
(Traditional quality clothing, shoes, and accessories)

BRUNO MAGLI
800/624-5430
(Designer shoes)

BURBERRYS LIMITED
800/284-8480
(Raingear, clothing, scarves, and fine leather goods)

BULGARI
800/BULGARI for catalogue and stores
(Fine jewelry and watches)

CALVIN KLEIN
800/223-6808
(Designer clothing and accessories)

CARLOS FALCHI
800/243-0624
(Leather and reptile accessories)

CAROLEE DESIGNS
800/227-6533
(Faux gold, pearl, and rhinestone jewelry)

CARTIER
800/CARTIER
(Fine jewelry and watches)

CHANEL BOUTIQUE
800/550-0005
(Designer clothing, accessories, and cosmetics)

CHARLES DAVID
310/348-5050
(Designer shoes)

CHRISTIAN DIOR JEWELRY
800/456-9444
(Faux jewelry)

CINER
212/947-3770
(Faux jewelry)

COACH
800/262-2411
(Handbags and other leather goods)

COLE·HAAN
800/488-2000
(Designer shoes and leather accessories)

CONVERSE/JACK PURCELL
800/428-2667
(Sneakers and sportswear)

COUNTRY ROAD AUSTRALIA
201/854-8400
(Clothing and accessories)

DAYTON HUDSON MARSHALL FIELD
800/292-2450
(Upscale department store)

DIEGO DELLA VALLE
800/457-8637
(Designer shoes; carries J. P. Tod)

DILLARD'S PARK PLAZA
800/DILLARD
(Upscale department store)

DOCKERS
800/DOCKERS
(Casual workwear and accessories)

DONNA KARAN/DKNY
800/231-0884
(Designer clothing and accessories)

EDDIE BAUER
800/426-8020
(Casual and outdoor wear and gear)

FENDI
800/336-4349
(Designer clothing, bags, and accessories)

FERRAGAMO
212/838-9470
(Designer clothing and accessories)

FILENE'S
617/357-2601
(Department store)

THE GAP
415/777-0250
(Clothing and accessories)

GARDENER'S EDEN
800/822-9600
(Gates Boot Company Wellingtons and other foul-weather shoes)

GERARD YOSCA
212/302-4349
(Jewelry)

GIORGIO ARMANI
201/570-1122
(Designer clothing and accessories)

GUCCI
800/234-8224
(Fine leather goods, shoes, and clothing)

HELEN KAMINSKI
800/291-3596
(Hats, straw bags, and other accessories)

HENRI BENDEL
212/247-1100
(Upscale specialty store)

HERMÈS
800/441-4488
(Fine leather goods, clothes, silk scarves, and jewelry)

HUSHPUPPIES
800/433-HUSH
(Casual shoes)

ISOTONER
800/410-1685
(Gloves)

ISAAC MIZRAHI
212/334-0055
(Designer clothing and ISAAC collection)

JC PENNEY
800/222-6161
(Clothing and accessories)

J. CREW
800/782-8244
(Sportswear and accessories)

JILL STUART
212/921-4161
(Designer clothing and accessories)

J. PETERMAN'S COMPANY'S OWNER'S MANUAL
800/231-7341
(Clothing and accessories)

JUDITH LEIBER
212/736-4244
(Designer handbags)

KANGOL
800/431-1802
(Hats)

KARA VARIAN BAKER
212/391-4450
(Jewelry)

KATE SPADE
212/279-2825
(Designer bags)

KEDS
800/428-6575
(Sneakers)

KENNETH JAY LANE
212/868-1780
(Faux jewelry)

LALIQUE
800/993-2580
(Glass jewelry and scarves)

LANDS' END
800/356-4444
(Sportswear for women)

LEEKAN DESIGNS, INC.
212/226-7226
(Ethnic jewelry, beads, and art objects)

L.L. BEAN RETAIL STORE
800/341-4341
(Outdoor wear and gear)

LEVI STRAUSS & CO.
800/USA-LEVI
(Denim and sportswear accessories)

THE LIMITED
614/479-2000
(Clothing and accessories)

LIZ CLAIBORNE
201/295-6650
(Designer clothing and accessories)

LORD & TAYLOR
212/391-3344
(Upscale specialty store)

LOUIS, BOSTON
800/225-5135
(Designer clothing and accessories)

LOUIS VUITTON
800/285-2255
(Designer clothing)

MACY'S (BULLOCK'S, AÉROPOSTALE)
800/45-MACYS
(Department store)

MARC JACOBS
212/343-0222
(Jewelry and clothing)

MARK CROSS
800/281-7716
(Fine bags and leather goods)

MARSHALL FIELD
800/292-2450
(Upscale department store)

MAXMARA/SPORTMAX
800/206-6872
(Clothing and accessories)

NATHALIE M.
310/348-5050
(Designer shoes)

NEIMAN MARCUS
800/937-9146
(Upscale department store)

NICOLE MILLER
800/365-4721
(Designer clothing and accessories)

NIKE
800/344-6453
(Activewear and sneakers)

NINA
800/233-NINA
(Shoes)

NORDSTROM
800/285-5800
(Upscale department store)

NORMA KAMALI
800/8-KAMALI
(Designer clothing and accessories)

OAKLEY
800/733-6255
(Sunglasses)

OLD NAVY
800/653-6289
(Classic sportswear and accessories from
the people who brought you The Gap)

OLIVER PEOPLES
310/657-5475
(Eyewear)

OPTICAL AFFAIRS
800/877-0655
(Eyewear)

PALOMA PICASSO
212/421-2260
(Leather bags and accessories; jewelry
exclusively sold through Tiffany & Co.)

PARISIAN
205/940-4000
(Department store)

PATAGONIA
800/638-6464
(Activewear and gear)

PAUL STUART
800/678-8278
(Classic clothing and accessories)

PLAZA TOO
800/972-4179
(Fashion shoes and accessories)

RALPH LAUREN/POLO
212/606-2100
(Designer clothing, accessories, and
activewear)

RAY·BAN
800/472-9226
(Sunglasses)

RHINESTEIN/ROSS
212/772-1901
(Fine jewelry)

RICH'S
404/913-4000
(Specialty store)

ROLEX
212/758-7700
(Watches)

ROBINSONS-MAY
800/633-1224
(Department store)

S & B REPORT
212/683-7612
($49 annual fee to receive monthly
mailer of designer sample sales in
New York City)

SAKS FIFTH AVENUE
212/753-4000
(Upscale department store)

SPIEGEL, INC.
800/345-4500
(Clothing and accessories)

STEPHANE KÉLIAN
212/925-3077
(Designer shoes)

STUSSY
212/274-8855
(Unisex sportswear and accessories)

**SUNGLASS HUT
INTERNATIONAL, INC.**
800/597-5005
(Sunglasses, all-purpose eyewear, and
sports brands)

**SUSAN BENNIS
WARREN EDWARDS**
800/634-9884
(Designer shoes)

SWATCH
800/937-9282
(Watches)

TAKASHIMAYA
800/753-2038
(Clothing and accessories, including
John Iverson)

TALBOTS
800/992-9010
(Clothing and accessories)

TARGET STORES
800/800-8800
(Upscale discounted merchandise)

TEMPLE ST. CLAIR CARR
212/219-8664
(Jewelry)

T. ANTHONY, LTD.
800/722-2406
(Fine leather accessories and luggage)

TIFFANY & CO.
212/605-4612
(Fine jewelry and accessories, including
Paloma Picasso's jewelry)

TIMEX
800/367-8463
(Watches, including Benetton, Joe Boxer,
Nautica, and Timberland)

URBAN OUTFITTERS
215/569-3131
(Casualwear and accessories)

VAN CLEEF & ARPELS
800/VCA-5797
(Fine jewelry)

VERDURA
212/265-3227
(Fine jewelry)

WATHNE
800/942-1166
(Elegant clothing, accessories, and
sporting gear)

YVES SAINT LAURENT
212/988-3821
(Designer clothing, scarves, shoes, and
accessories)

UNITED STATES

California

FRED SEGAL
8100 Melrose Avenue
Los Angeles, CA 90046
213/651-3342
(Specialty store)

L.A. EYE WORKS
7407 Melrose Avenue
Los Angeles, CA 90046
213/653-8255
(Eyewear)

STRADIVARI SHOES
1133 Montana Avenue
Santa Monica, CA 90403
310/394-3249
(Shoes)

Georgia

JERONIMO'S
3234 Roswell Road
Atlanta, GA 30305
404/233-3234
(Western wear and boots)

SKIPPY MUSKET
3500 Peachtree Road
Atlanta, GA 30326
404/233-3462
(Estate jewelry)

Maine

ANNE KLEIN OUTLET
Fashion Street Mall
Depot Street
Freeport, ME 04032
207/865-9555
(Discounted Anne Klein apparel)

CALVIN KLEIN OUTLET
11 Bow Street
Freeport, ME 04032
207/865-1051
(Discounted Calvin Klein apparel and accessories)

DONNA KARAN COMPANY STORE
42 Main Street, Suite #3
Freeport, ME 04032
207/865-1751
(Discounted Donna Karan apparel and accessories)

FOURTEEN CARROTS
Main Street
Northeast Harbor, ME 04662
207/276-5259
(Fine jewelry, handknit sweaters, and handwoven scarves)

J. CREW OUTLET
31 Main Street
Freeport, ME 04032
207/865-3180
(Discounted J. Crew apparel and accessories)

L.L. BEAN FACTORY STORE
150 High Street
Ellsworth, ME 04605
207/667-7753
(Sportswear and gear)

THE PATAGONIA OUTLET
9 Bow Street
Freeport, ME 04032
207/865-0506
(Discounted Patagonia activewear)

New Hampshire

L.L. BEAN FACTORY OUTLET
Route 16
North Conway, NH 03860
603/356-2100
(Discounted sportswear and gear)

New York

AARON FABER
666 Fifth Avenue
New York, NY 10103
212/586-8411
(20th-century fine jewelry and watches)

AD HOC
410 West Broadway
New York, NY 10012
212/925-2652
(Accessories)

AGNÈS B.
116 Prince Street
New York, NY 10012
212/925-4649
(Designer clothing and accessories)

A.P.C.
131 Mercer Street
New York, NY 10012
212/966-9685
(Designer clothing and accessories)

ARTWEAR
456 West Broadway
New York, NY 10012
212/673-2000
(Contemporary artisan jewelry)

BARRY KIESELSTEIN-CORD
5 East 57th Street
New York, NY 10022
212/754-6388
(Fine signature jewelry, belts, handbags)

BERGDORF GOODMAN
754 Fifth Avenue
New York, NY 10019
212/753-7300
(Upscale specialty store)

BIG DROP
134 Spring Street
New York, NY 10012
212/966-4299
(Funky clothing and accessories)

BILLY MARTIN'S WESTERN WEAR, INC.
812 Madison Avenue
New York, NY 10021
212/861-3100
(Westernwear and boots)

BUFFALO CHIPS
116 Greene Street
New York, NY 10012
212/274-0651
(Westernwear and boots)

CANAL JEANS
504 Broadway
New York, NY 10012
212/226-1130
(Casual clothing and accessories)

CELINE
51 West 57th Street
New York, NY 10022
212/308-6262
(French designer clothing and accessories)

CENTURY 21
22 Cortlandt Street
New York, NY 10007
212/227-9092
(Discounted clothing and accessories)

CULTURE & REALITY
59 Thompson Street
New York, NY 10012
212/431-1502
(Ethnic jewelry and clothing)

CYNTHIA ROWLEY
112 Wooster Street
New York, NY 10012
212/334-1144
(Designer clothing and accessories)

DETOUR
472 West Broadway
New York, NY 10012
212/979-6315
(Downtown clothes and accessories)

DOLLAR BILL
99 East 42nd Street
New York, NY 10017
212/867-0212
(Discount designer clothing)

ELIZABETH LOCKE AT PEIPERS + KOJEN
968 Madison Avenue
New York, NY 10021
212/744-7878
(Fine jewelry)

EMILIO PUCCI BOUTIQUE
24 East 64th Street
New York, NY 10021
212/752-8957
(Designer clothing and accessories)

ERIC SHOES
1333 Third Avenue
New York, NY 10021
212/288-8250
(Designer shoes)

FELISSIMO
10 West 56th Street
New York, NY 10019
212/956-4438
(Specialty store)

FRAGMENTS
107 Greene Street
New York, NY 10012
212/334-9588
(Jewelry, including Simon Tu and Cara Croninger)

FREELANCE
124 Prince Street
New York, NY 10012
212/925-6641
(Hip shoes)

GIORDANO'S
1118 First Avenue
New York, NY 10021
212/688-7195
(Petite shoes)

HENRI BENDEL
712 Fifth Avenue
New York, NY 10019
212/247-1100
(Specialty store)

H. KAUFFMAN & SONS SADDLERY
419 Park Avenue South
New York, NY 10016
212/684-6060
(Riding apparel and equipment)

INA
101 Thompson Street
New York, NY 10012
212/941-4757
(Designer resale shop)

INDUSTRIA
755 Washington Street
New York, NY 10014
212/366-4300
(Designer clothing and accessories)

JAMES ROBINSON
480 Park Avenue
New York, NY 10022
212/752-6166
(Estate jewelry)

J. M. WESTON
42 East 57th Street
New York, NY 10022
212/308-5655
(Hand-crafted men's shoes adapted for women)

KLEINBERG SHERRILL
35 East 65th Street
New York, NY 10021
212/772-3981
(Finely crafted buckles, belts, and handbags)

LA BAGAGERIE
727 Madison Avenue
New York, NY 10021
212/758-6570
(Bags and leather goods)

LAURENCE DEVRIES
207 West 16th Street
New York, NY 10011
212/633-1074
(Jewelry)

MANOLO BLAHNIK
15 West 55th Street
New York, NY 10019
212/582-1583
(Designer shoes)

MILLER HARNESS CO.
117 East 24th Street
New York, NY 10010
212/673-1400
(Riding apparel and equipment)

MORGENTHAL FREDERICS OPTICIANS
944 Madison Avenue
New York, NY 10021
212/744-9444
(Eyewear)

NORIKO MAEDA BOUTIQUE AT THE CARLYLE
985 Madison Avenue
New York, NY 10021
212/717-0330
(Elegant clothing and accessories)

PORTICO BED & BATH
139 Spring Street
New York, NY 10012
212/941-7722
(Sleep and bath wear)

PRADA
45 East 57th Street
New York, NY 10022
212/308-2332
(Designer clothing and accessories)

PRIVATE EYES
385 Fifth Avenue
New York, NY 10016
212/683-6663
(Eyewear, including Romeo Gigli)

REPLAY
109 Prince Street
New York, NY 10012
212/673-6300
(Italian designer jeans, clothing, and accessories)

ROBERT CLERGERIE
41 East 60th Street
New York, NY 10022
212/207-8600
(Designer shoes)

ROBERT LEE MORRIS
400 West Broadway
New York, NY 10012
212/431-9405
(Contemporary jewelry and leather accessories)

ROBERT MARC OPTICIANS
782 Madison Avenue
New York, NY 10021
212/737-6000 for stores
(Eyewear, including Freuden Haus)

SCREAMING MIMI'S
382 Lafayette Street
New York, NY 10003
212/677-6464
(Hip vintage clothing, hats, and faux jewelry)

SEAMAN SCHEPPS
485 Park Avenue
New York, NY 10022
212/753-9520
(Fine jewelry)

SEARLE
609 Madison Avenue
New York, NY 10022
212/753-9021
212/719-4610
(Designer clothing, outerwear, and accessories)

SELIMA OPTIQUE
59 Wooster Street
New York, NY 10012
212/343-9490
(Eyewear, including Alain Mikli, Karma Ricci, and Thierry Mugler)

STEVEN ALAN
60 Wooster Street
New York, NY 10012
212/334-6354
(Clothing and accessories, including Skagen watches, Hervé Chapelier bags, and Kate Spade bags)

STYLE LAB
64 East 7th Street
New York, NY 10003
212/505-3446
(Clothing and accessories)

TED MUELLING
47 Greene Street
New York, NY 10013
212/421-3825
(His signature jewelry)

TENDER BUTTONS
143 East 62nd Street
New York, NY 10021
212/758-7004
(Buttons and vintage cufflinks)

TIME WILL TELL
962 Madison Avenue
New York, NY 10028
212/861-2663
(Contemporary and antique watches)

TIP TOP SHOES
155 West 72nd Street
New York, NY 10023
212/787-4960
(Shoes, including Birkenstock)

TOOTSIE PLOHOUND
413 West Broadway
New York, NY 10012
212/925-3931
(Hip shoes)

**UNCLE SAM
UMBRELLA SHOP**
161 West 57th Street
New York, NY 10019
212/582-1976
(Quality umbrellas and repairs)

THE WATCH STORE
649 Broadway
New York, NY 10012
212/475-6090
(You guessed it)

ZONA
97 Greene Street
New York, NY 10012
212/925-6750
(Jewelry, including Spratling)

North Carolina

THE PHOENIX
Loblolly Pines
Duck, NC 27949
919/261-8900
(Clothing and accessories)

SHOES AT THE SQUARE
University Square
133 West Franklin Street
Chapel Hill, NC 27516
919/942-2044
(A wardrobe of shoes)

Oregon

CASSIE'S
22000 Willamette Drive
West Lynn, OR 97068
503/656-7141
(Clothing and accessories)

EL MUNDO
3556 SE Hawthorne
Portland, OR 97214
503/239-4605
(Clothing and accessories)

Pennsylvania

KNIT WIT
1721 Walnut Street
Philadelphia, PA 19103
215/564-4760
(Clothing and accessories)

MENDELSOHN
229 S. 18th Street
Philadelphia, PA 19103
215/546-6333
(Clothing and accessories)

PILEGGI ON THE SQUARE
717 Walnut Street
Philadelphia, PA 19106
215/627-0565
(Clothing and accessories)

TOBY LERNER
117 S. 17th Street
Philadelphia, PA 19103
215/568-5760
(Clothing and accessories)

Texas

LILY DATSUN
33 Highland Park Village
Dallas, TX 75205
214/528-0528
(Designer clothing and accessories)

STANLEY KORSHAK
500 Crescent Court
Dallas, TX 75201
214/871-3600
(Upscale specialty store)

Virginia

LEVYS
4925 West Broad Street
Richmond, VA 23230
804/354-1938
(Designer clothing and accessories)

OUT OF THE BLUE
2138 Barracks Road
Charlottesville, VA 22903
804/979-2583
(Eclectic clothing and accessories)

THE PHOENIX
3039 West Cary
Richmond, VA 23221
804/354-0711
(Clothing and accessories)

SCARPA
2114A Barracks Road
Charlottesville, VA 22903
804/296-0040
(Classic and contemporary shoes)

International Listings

AUSTRALIA

DAIMARU
21 La Trobe Street
Melbourne
3/660-6666
(Upscale department store)

DAVID JONES
Elizabeth Street
Sydney
2/266-5544
(Upscale department store)

GEORGES
162 Collins Street
Melbourne
3/283-5535
(Upscale department store)

**STEPHEN DAVIES
DESIGNER SHOES**
65 Gertrude Street, Fitzroy
Melbourne
3/419-6296
(Custom-made shoes)

DENMARK

MAGASIN DU NORD
Kongens Nytorv 13
1050 Copenhagen K
33/11-4433
(Upscale department store)

FRANCE

AGNÈS B.
3-6 rue du Jour
Paris 75001
0140/03-45-00
(Clothing and accessories)

AU PRINTEMPS
64 boulevard Haussmann
Paris 75009
0142/82-50-00
(Department store)

GALERIES LAFAYETTE
40 boulevard Haussmann
Paris 75009
0142/82-34-56
(Department store)

HERMÈS
24 rue du Faubourg-St.-Honoré
Paris 75002
0142/17-47-17
(Fine leather goods, clothes, silk scarves, and jewelry)

INÈS DE LA FRESSANGE
14 avenue Montaigne
Paris 75008
0147/23-08-94 or 0147/23-64-87
(Designer clothing and accessories)

ROBERT CLERGERIE
5 rue du Cherche-Midi
Paris 75006
0145/48-75-47
(Designer shoes)

STEPHANE KÉLIAN
26 avenue des Champs-Elysées
Paris 75008
0142/56-42-26
(Designer shoes; there are seven other boutiques in Paris)

GERMANY

LUDWIG BECK
Marienplatz 11
Munich
89/23-6910
(Upscale department store)

MEY & EDLICH
Theatinerstrasse 7
Munich
89/290-0590
(Upscale department store)

GREAT BRITAIN

AGNÈS B.
35–36 Floral Street
London WC2
171/379-1992
(Clothing and accessories)

BURBERRYS LIMITED
165 Regent Street
London W1
171/734-4060
(Raingear, clothing, scarves, and fine leather goods)

BUTLER AND WILSON
189 Fulham Road
London SW3
171/352-3045
(Faux jewelry)

CUTLER & GROSS
16 Knightsbridge Green
London SW1
171/581-2250
(Eyewear)

EMMA HOPE SHOES
33 Amwell Street
London EC1
171/833-2367
(Designer shoes)

THE GAP
31 Long Acre
London WC2
171/379-0779
(Clothing and accessories)

HARRODS
Knightsbridge
London SW1
171/730-1234
(Upscale department store)

HARVEY NICHOLS
109–125 Knightsbridge
London SW1
171/235-5000
(Scarves, jewelry, and hosiery)

HERMÈS
155 New Bond Street
London W1
171/499-8856
(Fine leather goods, clothes, silk scarves, and jewelry)

JONES
15 Floral Street
London WC2
171/379-4448
(Clothing and accessories)

KENZO
15 Sloane Street
London SW1
171/235-4021
(Clothing and accessories)

LIBERTY
210–222 Regent Street
London W1
171/734-1234
(Scarves, jewelry, belts, bags, and clothing)

MANOLO BLAHNIK
49–51 Old Church Street
London SW3
171/352-8622
(Designer shoes)

MUJI
26 Great Marlborough Street
London W1
171/494-1197
(Clothing and accessories)

PATRICK COX SHOES
8 Symons Street
London SW3
171/730-6504
(Designer shoes)

PAUL SMITH WOMEN
40–44 Floral Street
London WC2
171/379-7133
(Smart, hip fashion)

PRADA
44-45 Sloane Street
London SW1
171/235-0008
(Designer clothing and accessories)

ROBERT CLERGERIE
67 Wigmore Street
London W1
171/935-3601
(Elegant footwear)

SPACE NK LTD
41 Earlham Street
London WC2
171/379-7030
(Simple, modern clothing, shoes, and bags)

SWAINE, ADENEY, BRIGGS & SONS LTD
10A Old Barn Street
London, W1
171/409-7277
(Riding clothes and accessories)

ITALY

GIORGIO ARMANI
Via Sant'Andrea 9
Milan
2/7602-2757
(Designer clothing)

GUCCI
Via Condotti 8
Rome 00187
6/679-0405
(Fine shoes, bags, and accessories)

LA RINASCENTE
Piazza Duomo
Milan
2/7200-2210
(Department store)

PRADA
Galleria Vittorio Emanuele 63–65
Milan
2/876-979
(Designer clothing and accessories)

PUCCI
Palazzo Pucci
Via dei Pucci 6
Florence 50122
3955/28-3061
(Fine shoes, bags, and accessories)

JAPAN

ISETAN
3-14-1 Shinjuku
Shinjuku-ku
Tokyo
3/3352-1111
(Specialty store)

SPAIN

CORTE INGLES
Raimundo Fernandez Villaverde 79
Madrid
1/532-8100
(Upscale specialty store)

LOEWE
Calle Serrano 26
Madrid
1/435-0645
(Luxury leather goods)

RESOURCES

KAZUKO

If having a spiritual life seems beyond your grasp, consider stroking a crystal. Jewelry designer (and sometime actress and scarf designer) Kazuko believes that her self-dubbed "healing sculptures" of coral, pearls, semiprecious and precious stones wrapped in gold-filled wire magically conduit peace and well-being. And she has many loyal customers—including monologist/actor Spalding Gray and model Veruschka—who share that belief. Concert musicians wear her charms for luck, as do those who are scared of making gaffes while on television. Because of Kazuko's unorthodox production process, no two pieces turn out alike: "When I'm making the sculptures, I ask the wires to move for me. It's very serious concentration. I don't draw. I don't design. It just comes out of my heart." Kazuko's spiritual "transmitters" are available exclusively from Barneys worldwide. *(Barneys New York 800/777-0087)*

JUDITH LEIBER

This bag lady goes to black-tie functions. Judith Leiber has been bedecking the glamorous and wealthy (Beverly Sills, Kim Basinger, Pat Buckley, Ivana Trump, to name a few) with her jeweled, exotic, whimsical designs since 1963. Leiber has always been top-notch. The craftsmanship involved, which she herself learned within an artisan's guild in Budapest, is unparalleled. Her signature minaudières are covered with 7,000 to 13,000 pavé rhinestones, each individually handset. One bag can take up to seven days for an artisan to complete. *(Judith Leiber 212/736-4244)*

52 PADDOCK BOOTS—Imperial

53 YELLOW RUBBER BOOT—Gates Boot Company; **BLACK LEATHER BOOT**—Chanel

55 SUNGLASSES—Calvin Klein; **BLACK WATCH**—Swatch; **SILVER CUFF BRACELET, SILVER LINK BRACELETS,** and **SILVER RINGS**—Kara Varian Baker; **CELLULAR PHONE**—Motorola; **CELLULAR PHONE CASE**—T. Anthony; **BLACK NYLON BAG**—Gap; **BLACK SUEDE SNEAKERS**—Private collection of Adam Glassman; **BLACK POLISHED-LEATHER OXFORD SHOES**—J. M. Weston

61 BROWN LEATHER BAG—La Bagagerie; **YELLOW WOOD BAG**—Kleinberg Sherrill; **POLISHED-LEATHER BELT**—J. Crew

62 BROWN SUEDE PUMP—Manolo Blahnik at Barneys New York; **CHAIN AND LEATHER BELT**—Paloma Picasso; **SNAKE WATCH, COIN GOLD EARRINGS,** and **GOLD STONE RINGS**—Bulgari; **GOLD BRACELET**—Barneys New York

63 WESTERN BELT WITH ALLIGATOR STRAP—Buffalo Chips; **METALLIC PASTEL LEATHER BELT**—Ben-Amun; **BLACK SUEDE BELT WITH RHINESTONE BUCKLE**—Takashimaya; **SADDLE-LEATHER BELT WITH BRASS BUCKLE**—Ralph Lauren; **FAUX LEOPARD BELT WITH FAUX TORTOISESHELL BUCKLE**—Ben-Amun; **SILVER CONCHA BELT**—Buffalo Chips; **MULTICOLORED RHINESTONE BELT**—Kenneth Jay Lane; **WIDE SUEDE BELT**—WCM Belts

64 ALLIGATOR BELT WITH SILVER BUCKLE—Ralph Lauren; **BLACK PATENT-LEATHER BELT**—Two Blondes

65 SILVER ALLIGATOR BELT BUCKLE—Barry Kieselstein-Cord

66 BLACK POLISHED-LEATHER BAG—Gucci

68 BROWN LEATHER ACCORDION PURSE—Judith Leiber; **POLISHED-LEATHER BAG WITH BAMBOO HANDLE**—Gucci; **MINAUDIÈRE**—Judith Leiber; **YELLOW SILK-SATIN SHANTUNG DRAWSTRING EVENING POUCH**—Kate Spade

69 PIGSKIN KELLY BAG—Hermès; **BROWN SUEDE SOFT TOTE**—Sonoma Collection by Coach; **BROWN LEATHER AND GREEN NYLON SHOULDER BAG**—Wathne; **BLACK PLEATED SATIN CLUTCH WITH RHINESTONE CLASP**—Judith Leiber; **DRAWSTRING SHOULDER BAG**—Louis Vuitton; **BLACK NYLON BACKPACK**—Prada at Barneys New York; **CROCHETED STRAW BUCKET BAG**—Helen Kaminski

70 KHAKI WOOL GABARDINE SUIT—Paul Stuart. FIRST ENSEMBLE: **SILK SCARF**—Yves Saint Laurent; **FLORAL NECKLACE** and **BRACELET**—Mish; **ENAMEL SHELL EARRINGS** and **GOLD LINK BRACELET**—Seaman Schepps; **SUNGLASSES**—Optical Affairs; **FAUX CORAL CUFF**—Kenneth Jay Lane; **WHITE BAND WATCH**—Agatha; **LIGHT-PINK LEATHER TRAIN CASE**—Wathne; **BEIGE AND BLACK CAP-TOE FLATS**—Chanel

71 (from left to right) **KHAKI WOOL GABARDINE SUIT**—Paul Stuart. SECOND ENSEMBLE: **BLACK SILK SHIRT**—Donna Karan; **SILK POCKET SQUARE**—Private collection of Adam Glassman; **WOOD AND GOLD CUFF** and **MATCHING SHELL EARRINGS**—Seaman Schepps; **BLACK POLISHED-LEATHER BAG**—Fendi; **BLACK POLISHED-LEATHER BELT**—J. Crew; **BLACK GUNMETAL CHAIN BRACELET**—Robert Lee Morris; **BLACK POLISHED-LEATHER PUMPS**—Robert Clergerie. THIRD ENSEMBLE: **SILK SCARF**—Ralph Lauren; **EYEGLASSES**—Calvin Klein; **POLISHED-LEATHER DRAWSTRING BAG**—Barneys New York; **STAINLESS-STEEL AND GOLD TANK WATCH**—Cartier; **ANKLE BOOTS** and **BLACK POLISHED-LEATHER BELT**—J. Crew

72 POLISHED-LEATHER AND PATENT-LEATHER SLINGBACK SHOE, QUILTED LEATHER BAG, LEATHER AND QUILTED CAP-TOE BALLET FLAT, and ASSORTED FAUX PEARL, GOLD, AND RHINESTONE JEWELRY—Chanel

74 TIBETAN SILVER NECKLACE—Culture & Reality; **WOVEN SILVER HOOPS**—John Iverson at Takashimaya; **WIDE ETHNIC SILVER CUFFS**—Culture & Reality; **SILVER BRACELET**—Kara Varian Baker; **BLACK DRAWSTRING NYLON TOTE**—Prada at Barneys New York; **BLACK SUEDE PUMPS**—Manolo Blahnik; **BLACK SUIT**—DKNY

75 BLACK LEATHER HIGH-HEELED TASSEL LOAFER—Diego Della Valle; **ALLIGATOR TOTE**—Judith Leiber; **WOOL SHAWL**—Anichini; **SUNGLASSES**—Optical Affairs; **TANK WATCH**—Gucci; **GOLD EARRINGS** and **TOURMALINE GOLD RING**—Elizabeth Locke; **BLACK LACQUER AND PRECIOUS-STONE JAGUAR CUFF**—Verdura

76 SILVER MESH BAG, BLUE PLASTIC AND FAUX SILVER-BEADED BAG, and PURPLE PLASTIC TOTE—Bottega Veneta; **YELLOW PLASTIC TOTE**—Nicole Miller; **BLACK AND YELLOW NYLON HANDBAG**—Hervé Chapelier at Barneys New York

77 NYLON MESSENGER BAG—Globe, NYC

78 BUTTONS—Tender Buttons, NYC

79 SHIRT—Dolce and Gabbana; **TYPEWRITER KEY CUFFLINK**—Paul Smith

85 BROWN LEATHER GLOVES—Coach; STAINLESS-STEEL AND GOLD TANK WATCH—Cartier; GREEN STONE RING—Rhinestein Ross; COIN GOLD RING—Elizabeth Locke; AMBER AND GOLD LINK BRACELET—Seaman Schepps; GOLD LINK BRACELET—Elizabeth Locke; GOLD BANGLES—Galleria Lano

86 BLACK FEATHERED GLOVE—Takashimaya; WHITE POLARTEC GLOVE—Private collection of Adam Glassman

88 VINTAGE GOLD BRACELETS—James Robinson

91 ANTIQUE GOLD CHARM BRACELET—Terry Rogers

92 SILVER BAG—Ferragamo; MATTE GOLD-PLATED CUFF—Robert Lee Morris; CORK NECKLACE—Ex Ovo; GOLD SCARF—Adrienne Landau; PEARL AND GOLD EARRINGS—Temple St. Clair Carr; CLEAR ACRYLIC BANGLES—Cara Croninger; SCATTER FAUX-DIAMOND BANGLES—Marc Jacobs for Charles Turi; FAUX LEOPARD MULES—Manolo Blahnik

93 MATTE GOLD-PLATED CUFF—Robert Lee Morris; SILVER CUFF and ACRYLIC CUFF—Cara Croninger at Fragments

94 VENETIAN GLASS INTAGLIO, SAPPHIRE, AND GOLD BRACELET—Elizabeth Locke

96 (top to bottom) OYSTER-FACE STAINLESS AND GOLD WATCH—Rolex; STAINLESS-STEEL MINIMALIST-DESIGN WATCH—Skagen at Steven Alan; GOLD TANK WATCH WITH ALLIGATOR BAND—Cartier; STAINLESS-STEEL WATCH WITH FLEXIBLE BAND—Mercury by Timex; DIGITAL WATCH—Ironman by Timex

97 WATCHES—(top to bottom) Artisan, Olympic Commemorative, and Classic by Swatch

98 TRICOLOR GOLD ROLLING RING—Cartier

99 CRYSTAL CABOCHON RINGS—Lalique

105 WOOL BERET—Kangol; WOOL CHALLIS SCARF—Yves Saint Laurent; SILVER DRAGONFLY PIN—Noosa Spratling; SUNGLASSES—Calvin Klein; SILVER EARRINGS—Laurence Devries; SEED AND SILVER NECKLACE—Ex Ovo

106 FUR and STRAW HATS—Darcy Creech

107 BASEBALL CAPS—Private collection of Jeff Stone

110 RAYON CREPE BLACK DRESS—MaxMara

JAMES ROBINSON

In 1912, James Robinson founded his eponymous store specializing in antique silver and antique Chinese porcelains. Today the business is still family owned and run by the founder's nephew, who has broadened the store's scope to include an extensive selection of art deco and antique twentieth-century jewelry and English and French porcelains and glass. James Robinson is perhaps most renowned for its handmade sterling silverware reproductions, crafted in the eighteenth-century tradition.

(James Robinson 212/752-6166)

111 SUNGLASSES—Christian Roth for Optical Affairs; BLACK LACE AND STRAW HAT—Takashimaya; FAUX PEARLS—Gerard Yosca; BLACK PEAU DE SOIE SHOES—Yves Saint Laurent; ALLIGATOR CLUTCH—Judith Leiber; FAUX PEARL EARRINGS—Miriam Haskell at Barneys New York

112 BLACK RAYON CREPE DRESS—MaxMara. RELAXED ENSEMBLE: BLACK SUNGLASSES—Christian Roth for Optical Affairs; SILVER PENDANT—John Iverson at Takashimaya; SILVER CUFF BRACELETS—Cara Croninger at Fragments; BLACK PATENT-LEATHER SANDALS—Birkenstock. POLISHED ENSEMBLE: FAUX PEARL EARRINGS—Mish; FAUX PEARL NECKLACE—Gerard Yosca; BLACK RAYON CREPE BELT—Max Mara; GOLD LINK BRACELET—Elizabeth Locke; BLACK QUILTED-LEATHER HANDBAG—Chanel; BLACK PUMPS—Barneys New York

113 BLACK RAYON CREPE DRESS—MaxMara. LUNCH ENSEMBLE: BLACK SUNGLASSES, SILVER HOOP EARRINGS, and BLACK PLASTIC CUFFS—Agatha; BLACK SCARF—Wathne; BLACK NYLON TOTE—Prada from Barneys New York; SILVER AND EBONY CUFF—Ex Ovo; BLACK POLISHED-LEATHER BELT—J. Crew; BLACK CAP-TOE PUMPS—Chanel. DINNER ENSEMBLE: GOLD HOOP EARRINGS and CHARM BRACELET—Provate collection of Adam Glassman; BLACK LEATHER HANDBAG—Paloma Picasso; BLACK PATENT-LEATHER SANDALS—J. Crew; GOLD LINK BELT—Paloma Picasso; BLACK SUEDE PUMPS—Anne Klein

114 BLACK VELVET SCULPTURED BAG WITH BAKELITE HANDLE—Paloma Picasso; FAUX GOLD AND ENAMEL BEE PIN—Carolee Designs

115 RED RHINESTONE AIDS PIN—James Arpad; GOLD AND PEARL BOW PIN—Carolee Designs

117 HEART and STAR CLUSTER PINS—Marc Jacobs; DIAMOND AND GOLD FLORAL PIN—Van Cleef & Arpels; FAUX PEARL CHOKER—Gerard Yosca; MARCASITE HUMMINGBIRD PIN—Vintage Creations; SEMIPRECIOUS STONE AND CRYSTAL BEADS AND GOLD-FILLED WIRE KILT PIN—Kazuko at Barneys New York

119 BLACK SATIN BOW—Riviera

120 OVERSIZED FAUX TORTOISESHELL HAIR PIN—Colette Malouf; FAUX TORTOISESHELL HAIR BAND, BARRETTE, and SCRUNCHY—Riviera; HAIR ELASTIC—Goody

121 LIPSTICK—Orlane; ATOMIZER—Muji; COMPACT—Private collection of Hope Greenberg

123 FAUX GRAY PEARL AND GLASS BEAD CLUSTER—Dana Kellin; FAUX PEARL SURROUNDED BY GOLD COILS—Kenneth Jay Lane; BAROQUE PEARL AND GOLD-WIRE EARRINGS—Private collection of Amanda Manogue Burch; FAUX PEARL SURROUNDED BY PAVÉ RHINESTONES—Kenneth Jay Lane; FAUX MABÉ PEARL EARRINGS—Christian Dior; GOLD HOOPS WITH SINGLE PEARL DROPS—Gabriella Sanchez; FAUX PEARL STUD EARRINGS—Ralph Lauren; FRESHWATER PEARL CLUSTER EARRINGS—Simon Tu at Fragments

J. M. WESTON

In the nineteenth century, American shoe manufacturing was considered the best in the Western world. Though the Blanchards' business was thoroughly French, the family renamed their company for the most American-sounding imaginary person they knew, J. M. Weston. Since 1865, J. M. Weston has represented the classic standard. Each shoe is constructed (in 75 steps) to last a lifetime. The quality is in the details: the cowhide used for the soles is cured in spring water for more than eight months; cork (ideal for insulation and water-resistance) lines every sole; and the arch support is a sliver of beechwood. Although only five styles are available for women, any shoe can be special-ordered. (*J. M. Weston 212/308-5655*)

124   **TOP SILVER HOOP**—Zina at Fragments; **FAR-RIGHT GOLD HOOP**—Trifari; **MIDDLE-RIGHT GOLD HOOP**—Carolee; **LARGE MIDDLE GOLD HOOP**—Erwin Pearl; **MIDDLE-LEFT GOLD HOOP**—Monet; **FAR-LEFT GOLD HOOP**—Monet; **LOWER-MIDDLE SILVER HOOP**—Monet; **BOTTOM SILVER HOOP**—Zina at Fragments

125   **MATTE GOLD-PLATED EARRING**—Robert Lee Morris

126   **DIAMOND NECKLACE**—Stephen Russell

127   **ZIRCONIA AND SILVER EARRING**—Ralph Lauren

129   **SATIN-FINISH METAL**—Romeo Gigli at Private Eyes; **FAUX BUFFALO HORN**—Freuden Haus at Robert Marc; **MULTI-COLORED ACETATE AND WIRE FRAME**—Selima Optique; **BLACK ACETATE**—Ray•Ban

130   **FAUX MOTHER-OF-PEARL SUN-GLASSES**—Mary McFadden for Renaissance; **BLACK PATENT-LEATHER CASE**—Thierry Mugler at Selima Optique; **PEARL EYEGLASS CHAIN**—Karma Ricci at Selima Optique

131   **SILVER WRAPAROUND SUNGLASSES**—Oakley

132   **SILK SCARF**—Hermès

134   **WHITE T-SHIRT**—Agnès B.; **COTTON PAREO**—Hermès

136   **WHITE PATENT-LEATHER FLORAL BAG**—Carlos Falchi; **SCARF**—Private collection of Adam Glassman; **SILK CAMELLIA PIN**—Chanel; **GOLD FLORAL EARRINGS**—Tiffany & Co.

137   **WHITE LEATHER TOTE** and **SPECTATOR SANDALS**—Bottega Veneta; **BLUE-AND-WHITE-STRIPED SCARF**—Ralph Lauren; **GOLD TANK WATCH WITH ALLIGATOR STRAP**—Cartier; **GOLD BRACELETS**—Galleria Cano; **GOLD EARRINGS**—Fragments, NYC

138   **GOLD-COLLAR NECKLACE**—Carlo Weingrill

139   **MATTE GOLD-PLATED NECK RING**—Robert Lee Morris

141   **BLACK LEATHER TOTE BAG**—Takashimaya; **WATCH**—Rolex; **BLACK POLISHED-LEATHER BELT**—Gucci; **BLACK POLISHED-LEATHER SHOES**—J. Crew; **WIRE SUNGLASSES**—Calvin Klein; **STERLING-SILVER CIRCLE-CHAIN BRACELET**—Tanah Kalb; **ANGEL RINGS DIAMOND-AND-PLATINUM NECKLACE**—Isaac Mizrahi; **STERLING-SILVER CUFF** and **STERLING SILVER-WITH-TURQUOISE BRACELETS**—Laurence Devries

142–3   **METALLIC SCARF**—Adrienne Landau; **AUSTRIAN GLASS BEADS**—Cathy Fabrikant; **EARRINGS**—Dana Kellin; **SILVER CUFFS**—Robert Lee Morris; **CRYSTAL CABOCHON RINGS**—Lalique; **BLACK PLEATED SILK BAG WITH STONE CLASP**—Judith Leiber; **SILVER MESH MULES**—Bernard Figueroa

144   **PEARLS**—CIRO

147   **JACKIE O NECKLACE**—Kenneth Jay Lane

KATE SPADE

Just because bags are handy to hold stuff doesn't meant they can't be irreverent while on the job. Ever since 1993, when former accessories editor Kate Spade started up her company (with her college sweetheart and business partner, Andy Spade), picking out a handbag has gotten a lot more fun. Unlike most of Seventh Avenue, Spade is not afraid of color: she embraces a vibrant, off-beat palette. And better still, the collection's minimalist designs harken back to a retro-flea-market stylistic mood. Spade keeps prices down by using seasonal fabrics—linen, canvas, novasuede, nylon, satin, wool melton—not leather. And in February 1996, Spade's line received the industry's highest honor: the Council of Fashion Designers of America's Perry Ellis Award for New Fashion Talent in accessories design. (*Kate Spade 212/279-2825*)

QUOTES

TENDER BUTTONS

Longtime button enthusiasts Diana Epstein and Millicent Safro have been proprietors of this Upper East Side institution since they took over the eclectic inventory in 1964. Renaming the establishment Tender Buttons (for the little-known Gertrude Stein work), this miniature emporium quickly became a mecca for button collectors, fashion designers, and anyone interested in giving his or her clothes a makeover. Epstein and Safro are now experts in the field: they have curated shows on buttons at the Smithsonian Institution in Washington, D.C., and the Gallery at the Ginza in Tokyo, and have lectured at the Cooper-Hewitt Museum. They do museum and private appraisals and supervise the factory production of their own designs. They have also produced a book (called—what else?—*Buttons*) on the subject that concerns us all (except the button-eschewing Amish) as we dress ourselves every morning. (*Tender Buttons* 212/758-7004)

CHIC SIMPLE STAFF

PARTNERS Kim & Jeff
ART DIRECTOR Wayne Wolf
ASSOCIATE EDITOR Victoria C. Rowan
ASSOCIATE ART DIRECTOR Alicia Yin Cheng
OFFICE MANAGER Joanne Harrison
COPY EDITOR Borden Elniff

ACKNOWLEDGMENTS

ACCESSORIES CONSULTANT Lisa Wertheimer-Wells RESEARCH ASSISTANT Heather Starr SPECIAL THANKS TO: Barneys New York, David Bashaw, Jean Berschens, Paul Bogaards, Claire Bradley, Gabrielle Brooks, Amy Capen, Robin Cavan, Althea Cox, Franc Cussoneau, Anna DeLuca, Damian Donck, Richela Fabian, Jane Friedman, Hedy Gold, Dr. Lloyd Hoffman, Kate Doyle Hooper, Andy Hughes, Carol Janeway, Gia Kim, Nicholas Latimer, Dr. Suzanne M. Levine, Julie Livingston of the World Gold Council, Bill Loverd, Brenda Lynn, Dwyer McIntosh, Sonny Mehta, Anne Messitte, Kay Morrow, Christine Notaro, Carla Phillips, Lynn Ramsey of the Jewelry Information Center, Mona Reilly, Tracy Rose, Mitchell Rosenbaum, Amy Schuler, Takuyo Takahashi, Shelley Wanger, Amy Zenn.

INVALUABLE RESOURCES

Annette Tapert and Diana Edkins, *The Power of Style* (Crown, 1994); Peggy Crisman and Shirley Worley, *Bead Talk* (Beads Unique, 1993); Leah Feldon, *Dress Like a Million (On Considerably Less)* (Villard, 1993); International Gemological Institute, New York; Alison Lurie, *The Language of Clothes* (Vintage, 1981); Harold Newman, *An Illustrated Dictionary of Jewelry* (Thames and Hudson, 1981); Georgia O'Hara, *The Encyclopedia of Fashion* (Abrams, 1986); New York Public Library Information Service.

COMMUNICATIONS

Chic Simple is about information, and you the reader are one of our conduits to that information. Since the publication of our first books, the letters, e-mail, and faxes have pointed out everything from typos to unique stores or products from all over the globe. With your feedback have come suggestions on new titles for us to explore, and this book was the end result—so thanks for helping create the first Chic Simple title by request. A lot of the questions we get are about what else is in the series, so we created a catalogue. If you would like to receive one for free, please send us a pair of ruby-red slippers or your address, whichever is handier, to:

CHIC SIMPLE
84 WOOSTER STREET, NEW YORK, NY 10012
Fax: (212) 343-9678
Compuserve number: 72704,2346
E-mail address: info@chicsimple.com
Website address: http://www.chicsimple.com
Stay in touch because . . .
"The more you know, the less you need."

Please let us know if you're interested in Chic Simple clothing patterns, and let us know what your favorite accessory is.

A NOTE ON THE TYPE

The text of this book was set in New Baskerville and Futura. The ITC version of NEW BASKERVILLE is called Baskerville, which itself is a facsimile reproduction of types cast from molds made by John Baskerville (1706–75) from his designs. Baskerville's original face was one of the forerunners of the type style known to printers as the "modern face"—a "modern" of the period 1800. FUTURA was produced in 1928 by Paul Renner (1878–1956), former director of the Munich School of Design, for the Bauer Type Foundry. Futura is simple in design and wonderfully restful to read. It has been widely used in advertising because of its even, modern appearance in mass and its harmony with a great variety of other modern types.

SEPARATION AND FILM PREPARATION BY
COLOR SYSTEMS, INC.
New Britain, Connecticut

PRINTED AND BOUND BY
BERTELSMANN PRINTING AND
MANUFACTURING CORP.
Berryville, Virginia

HARDWARE

Power PC 9500, 8100, Apple Macintosh Power PC 8100, Quadra 800 personal computers; APS Technologies Syquest Drives; Iomega Zip Drive; MicroNet DAT drive; SuperMac 21-inch color monitor; Radius PrecisionColor Display/20; Radius 24X series video board; QMS 1660 Printer; Hewlett-Packard LaserJet 4, Supra fax modem.

SOFTWARE

QuarkXPress 3.3, Adobe Photoshop 2.5.1, Microsoft Word 5.1, FileMaker Pro 2.0, Adobe Illustrator 5.0.1.

MUSICWARE

Raga Aberi *(Shanker)*, Chet Baker *(Somewhere Over the Rainbow)*, Greg Brown *(The Live One)*, Maria Callas *(La Divina 2)*, Patsy Cline *(The Patsy Cline Story)*, Duke Ellington & John Coltrane, Exotica *(Motion Picture Sountrack)*, Ella Fitzgerald *(The Best of the Songbooks 1 and 2)*, Red Garland *(All Kinds of Weather)*, Juliette Gréco *(Gréco Chante Mac Orlan)*, Latin Playboys *(Latin Playboys)*, Leaving Las Vegas *(Motion Picture Soundtrack)*, Bruce Springsteen *(The Ghost of Tom Joad* and *Nebraska)*, Sarah Vaughn *(The George Gershwin Songbook)*.

"To my mind, simplicity is the keynote
of all true elegance."

COCO CHANEL